THE DEFINITIVE GUIDE TO CHOOSING A NURSERY

Jane E. Smalley

About This Book

This book has been written to provide a clear and definitive guide for parents seeking day nursery care for their baby, toddler or child. It provides the reader with a clear picture of what a good nursery should look like and what to look out for. Once read, the book will prepare parents for the first visit to a nursery with a check list of questions to ask and observations to make. In short, reading this book will be like having an expert on hand whenever you visit a nursery.

Dedications

For my beloved Graeme, thank you for believing in me and in this book.

Also

For my mother, for everything.

Contents

Preface

I have chosen to write this book as a practical guide to parents who may be considering using a private day nursery to care for their child on returning to work, or for those parents who already use a day nursery for their child and would like to find out more about the care their child is receiving.

I hope too that day care providers may find the book useful in trying, firstly, to identify if the care they currently provide is 'outstanding', 'good' or 'needs improving' and, secondly, as a self-evaluation tool for making improvements and for completing the Self Evaluation Form (SEF).

As an Early Years Education Consultant/Trainer and Nursery Teacher I have spent large portions of my time driving across England visiting and providing guidance, advice and training to providers of day care. I have visited, literally, hundreds of nurseries over the last ten years and have witnessed care that ranges from awful to good. Some of the nurseries I visit are, in my opinion, adequate though they may have achieved a 'good' or better grade than this from Ofsted. Ofsted is the Government-appointed body to inspect all private, voluntary and statutory (PVS) establishments which provide care/education for children 0-nineteen years.

Does this mean that we cannot trust the grade given to a setting by Ofsted? The answer to this is complex. A nursery inspection will take place only once every three years for some settings. Nurseries and staff will know what to do to achieve a 'good' grade and know how to perform on the day. Ofsted inspect against a set of welfare requirements. These lay down the minimum standard of care each child and family can expect. Inspectors will observe the behaviour and attitudes of staff, they will assess the quality of the environment available for children to access and they will check the organisational procedures of the setting. This will normally take place on the same day.

Many nurseries are providing exactly that, a minimum standard of care and are happy to settle for that.

In short, the grade a setting achieves on inspection is important but what really determines the quality and type of care on offer to a child will be determined by the attitudes of the owner/manager and staff.

An owner/manager who tells me that, 'We're quite happy, we achieved a 'good' on inspection' is of concern to me. I always counter this with, 'Oh dear, I am sorry, but now we can use that as a starting point to achieve 'outstanding''.

When speaking or delivering training I explain it like this; when we are content with a 'good' what we are really saying is that it is OK for children to experience a good-enough standard of care and nurture. Well I don't know about you, but I most certainly did not bring my children up to experience anything less than an 'outstanding' experience of life.

Many of my clients, both owners and managers, want that too. They want children to have what they would want for their own children. They want to achieve 'outstanding' from Ofsted. I help them with that, but many of the suggestions for change or training I make are not Ofsted requirements. They are actually suggestions for creating the very highest possible quality of care and education for every child and family.

So why is it so difficult to provide 'outstanding' care every day; what's the problem? For children to receive an 'outstanding' experience everyone who works with children must want this too. From the cleaner to the cook and the person who buys the weekly groceries. Everyone must want the very best for each and every child. And that is the problem. Some of the people who work in nurseries with children are not always the most suitable people. Some of these people are there by default. They may be there because they have been told that they were, 'no good' at school by teachers or parents. Some may have spent their leisure time babysitting for family members, even missing school to do so and now feel that minding children is the one thing they can do. Some may have studied childcare qualifications because they were unable to get onto the study course of their choice. They may have been directed to childhood studies by a well-meaning careers advisor because the young school-leaver lacked any real academic ability and childcare is 'just playing'.

'I really love kids' is not a reason for working with children and neither is under-achievement at school, harsh though that may sound. We really need dedicated, mature, experienced adults who are genuinely interested in working with children. We need adults in the industry who are willing to commit to further study and training in this exciting field.

Let us pause for a moment and reflect on the fact that today, following the tragic death of Victoria Climbié and Lord Laming's subsequent inquiry and report, 'Every Child Matters' became the government agenda for children. This program identifies the five outcomes for children. Each and every organisation that has contact with children or young people must ensure that they strive to help children to achieve in these five areas: 'being healthy', 'staying safe', 'enjoying and achieving', 'making a positive contribution' and 'economic well-being'. 'Every Child Matters' applies to every child from birth to nineteen years of age. Yes nineteen years of age! I find it difficult, therefore, to reconcile myself to the idea that in some of our nurseries we have very young men and women (under nineteen years of age) looking after societies' most vulnerable group. I believe these young people, who are still growing and developing their own characteristics, strengths and personalities, are in need of help, support and mentoring as they progress from teenage to adolescence. I am not suggesting that there is no place for young, qualified and enthusiastic men and women in our nurseries; after all anyone who has had to keep up with a toddler for eight hours a day knows how much energy it requires. But if young people are to be employed in our nurseries let us provide the mentoring and support they need from mature colleagues until they are deemed ready to take sole responsibility of very young children. At this time I am not aware of any nursery that offers this type of support to young staff.

Occasionally, following an intense period of in-house training with a nursery I have seen staff resign their post. This is something I have forewarned the owner/manager about. Whenever staff have left it has always been those staff members that the nursery wanted to lose.

Why does this happen? Because when I begin to train adults, asking them to view the world from the child's position, this may prove challenging for some people. They may have to acknowledge that their long-held beliefs and behaviours are no longer acceptable. It may challenge the way in which they were parented or how they currently parent their own child.

People choosing to work in this field need to take a long, hard look at why they came into childcare and what they can bring to each child's experience every day.

I am writing this book also because, so often, having visited a really poor nursery, I have asked myself this question, 'How can people leave their children here?'

But the answer is that many parents do not have a very clear guide about what is good and what is bad practice. Also parents do not have the luxury of being able to spend hours each week watching practitioners at work, as I have. Even if they did I fear that many, though not happy with what they have seen, will not know what may be acceptable or unacceptable practice.

Worryingly I have come across staff in nurseries, and some parents, who really don't know a great deal about the needs of small children. This is a serious concern when it comes to staff as they should know, they should be reading and studying the latest research and observing children regularly to inform their practice.

When it comes to parents, well it is a different story; a baby arrives without a manual and many of us will get by with a little advice and by using our intuition. And this is fine because good parents have something the professional does not, a deep and unconditional love for their child. So when we make mistakes, as even good parents do, the repercussions are often not too terrible. But we must not allow our children to be subject to the mistakes and poor standards of care day-in and day-out at the hands of those entrusted to care for them.

Choosing the right day care is not easy. This book is here to help, you but before we move on let's consider another type of care available today; childminding, which is covered in more detail in Chapter 15. Childminders are people who care for other people's children in their own home. All childminders should be registered with the Local Authority (LA) in which they live and work. Do not use a childminder who is unable to show you his/her Ofsted registration document, insurance certificate or evidence of planning. All childminders must be inspected by Ofsted within six months of being registered.

Note.

For ease of writing I have referred to staff in the female and children in the male gender terms.

About the Author

Jane Smalley was born in Birkenhead, the middle child in a family of ten children. Jane's early childhood was spent playing in the streets and on the banks of the River Mersey with her brothers and sisters. Jane's education really began, as a 30 year old mother of four children, when she enrolled at a local college of education and began a course of study in childcare. The people she met and the lecturers who taught her inspired her to continue her education over the next two decades. At 40 years of age Jane qualified as a teacher and began a career in lecturing in Childhood Studies. Five years later Jane opened her Consultancy and Training Academy, Nurserywise which she ran until 2010. Jane relocated to Shropshire in 2011 and taught at a prestigious independent school before opening Shrewsbury Prepatoria in January 2014. Shrewsbury Prepatoria is the UK's first and most comprehensive approach to Reggio Emilia education and seeks to redefine education and care for children under five years of age.

About this Book

This book is the culmination of 35 years' experience of working with children, initially as a parent and childminder and finally as a professional. Latterly my career provided me with an incredible opportunity to witness, first-hand the quality of education and care available today to societies' most vulnerable group, the under-fives. It is my experience, as an Early Years Consultant and Trainer, that led to this book being written but it is impossible to separate these experiences from my extensive knowledge, derived from years of study, and my in-depth understanding of children. As an Early Years Consultant I was invited to observe and assess literally hundreds of nurseries up and down the country. I spent countless hours observing the practice of childcare practitioners, spoke with and supported managers and assessed environments for children. Once observations were complete my role was to write a report. This report identified the changes necessary to raise the quality of education and care. A fully integrated training package for all team members would be put in place. This involved writing bespoke training programmes, which I delivered in-house, working alongside practitioners, to support changes to their practice. Every nursery I worked with improved their grade at the next Ofsted inspection.

There are two main aims of this book, the first is to provide parents with sufficient information about nurseries to make an informed choice. I aim to do this by telling you a little about what children really need.

Note, I do not aim to tell you what to do, there are plenty of books that will tell you how to bring up your baby! My aim is to give you food for thought, to provide you with information so that the decisions you make for your child are made thoughtfully and with the best information available at the time. The book takes you on a very logical journey from thinking about what your child needs, to deciding the type of care you want, to the first visit and the questions you should ask. I will explain what is deemed good practice and what is not so good and each chapter ends with a brief summary of the salient points. Easy to use sections throughout allow you to take the book with you on your visits or tours, providing space for you to make notes along the way. Though you will probably want to do this in the car and not whilst questioning the staff! I have included information about the Settling-in Period and the Key Person Role. Finally, there is a section on additional information which explains in a little more detail some of the jargon and terminology used in the book. In short, I hope that when you visit a nursery for the first time you will feel confident, informed and prepared to ask meaningful questions supported by the 'expert in your pocket'

The second aim is to replicate my consultancy role, albeit in a written and condensed form, for day care practitioners and managers, who wish to assess their current practice and make changes necessary to raise the quality of education and care to all children in their setting. The book, in particular the Self-Assessment Tables and Chapter 9 onwards, will support continuous professional development (CPD) for all staff.

How to Use This Book

Parents:

New parents considering the day care needs of their small child are recommended to read the book through from beginning to end. This is because the book has been written primarily with you in mind. I have tried to cover all the areas you should give thought to before you begin to look for a nursery for your child or baby. The book moves logically on from your first visit to a nursery, questions you should ask, what you should observe in each room to a section with additional information. At the end of each chapter there is a summary and, where applicable, a set of questions you should ask or a space for notes for you to complete following the visit.

If you are looking for a nursery for your baby don't be tempted to read only the parts of the book that apply to babies. As your baby grows and develops he will move through each of the areas of the nursery encountering the different members of staff and accessing resources available there. If you love the baby room but feel less than happy about the space toddlers or pre-school children access you should take this into consideration. Naturally you will focus your time and questions on finding out more about what sort of care and attention your baby will receive, but you will have the book to refer to over time as your child moves through the nursery environment and life.

If you are the parent of an older child going back to work for the first time in two years or more then you may still wish to read the book as a whole. You may decide to skip Chapter 10, The Baby Room, but I suggest that you don't. I suggest you read the requirements for babies and then have a look at how the nursery actually do this. Ask, 'Are the very youngest children being cared for in a way I would have wanted my baby to be cared for'? Of particular importance to you may be Chapter 7, The Settling-in Period. If you have been at home with your child for the last two years or more it is very likely that your child will take much longer to settle-in than if they were a baby.

The book will also provide all parents with a valuable source of reference material to go back to time and again. It is highly unlikely that you will register your child with a nursery at six months of age and leave at some point before he is five years of age and never have any questions, doubts or concerns at all. When you do have questions or doubts, re-read the book, talk to the manager, chat to other parents and don't stop until you are satisfied. Remember you are your child's advocate. If you have chosen the right setting for your child then they will be happy to work with you to understand your concerns and be willing to address them. Occasionally I have heard parents of children in nurseries and in school say that they, 'didn't want to cause a fuss' or that they felt if they spoke out about concerns, in some way the teacher would, 'take it out' on the child. As a nursery and reception class teacher I can tell you that I have had to deal with a great many concerns, questions and sometimes complaints from parents over the years. Most of these I completely understood from the parent's perspective and worked hard with parents to find a solution. On very few occasions in my past career and in my present role, have I actually encountered a parent who was 'difficult' but in each situation I have simply applied my professional knowledge and expertise to work to find a solution. Never, has a parent's attitude, behaviour or request had a detrimental effect on the relationship I have had with a child and, more importantly, I have never heard a colleague or practitioner tell me it had either.

At the end of the book there are a set of Tables for Self-Assessment, these tables have been designed for use by and are of particular value to experienced childcare practitioners or managers. Having read the book you may find some of the content in the tables useful too.

Day Care Practitioners and Managers:

As indicated, I have worked for many years with some wonderful professionals who really want to create a nurturing and exciting environment for children. People who have invested vast amounts of time, money and energy to do so. To those practitioners and managers who consistently strive to attain an 'outstanding' grade from Ofsted, and once achieved, never cease to develop their practice I urge you to read the book through rather than going directly to the Self-Assessment tables at the back. If you do this it may be that the tables will be read out of context. Scan the first couple of chapters, at least, to gain that valuable perspective. See your setting from the parent's or outsider's view. When you do come to the tables, use them as a diagnostic tool to assess the current situation. The statements will then become a set of goals to be worked through systematically. Downloadable copies are available on my website so why not print off a copy for each staff member or for each room to look through? You could ask room leaders to use the tables as a quick assessment tool. Ask staff to take a good look at each area, give a really honest score to each statement and bring that back for discussion at a full staff meeting for feedback.

Occasionally staff may feel that any activity which requires them to score, evaluate or assess their current practice is a challenge to their professionalism. When professionals feel like this it is difficult to have an honest, open discussion that supports development and growth. There are a number of things that can be done to mitigate the negative impact of using any diagnostic or assessment tool. The kind of manager you are will affect the way in which your staff team approach any sort of assessment. How to manage day care is a topic all on its own and we don't have time for that here, so for now here are a few ideas about how to introduce this to the staff.

Give everyone a copy of the tables at a staff meeting, tell them you have just found these on-line and ask if people think they could be helpful at all. Allow people to moan, complain or discuss their thoughts, then ask for a volunteer to try them out to and give feedback to colleagues at the next staff meeting.

Alternatively, you could share some of the ideas from this book at a staff meeting and show the tables; admit that you want to support further change as you feel there is more you could do. Give everyone a copy of the tables, ask them to read them and to think through ways in which you could support them to make any changes they would **like** to make. In this way you are saying, 'I want to be better, I'm not afraid of assessment, I want change'.

Whatever you decide to do, it is important to keep your staff on board. My mantra, 'My team is my best asset' is forgotten at my own peril.

Chapter 1

What Do Children Really Need?

Our children are our children for such a short time. They come into our lives willing and wanting to have a relationship with us, their parents. They want to spend time with us. They look to us for guidance, fun and adventure.

Every day in the United Kingdom hundreds of thousands of small children are taken from their homes and transported to private day care or childminding homes to be looked after by paid carers. In nurseries children are separated into age ranges and placed in groups of, perhaps, as many as 20 other small children in a room they may only leave once or twice each day. In some nurseries they will be cared for by very young women or men who have never had a child and have little life experience. By the time the child is five years of age he or she may have had as many as 15 different carers. This care will vary enormously, the quality of which is dependent upon the nursery and the staff.

By the time the child is five years of age they must be formally educated and so for the next 11 years our children's lives, and our own, will be at the dictate of the education system. What time we rise each morning, when we holiday and what your child will learn is all decided for us.

It is my feeling, and great sadness, that childhood is becoming extinct and the small child and baby has almost become invisible in the community.

If we really want to know what is best for children then we have only to look at nature and what nature intended for our children.

Nature designed women to give birth, to just one baby or twins at any one time. We know this because this is what happens in the majority of cases. Of course some women give birth to triplets, but this is unusual. Why just one or two babies? Well, let us look at the way nature has shaped the human being. We have just two arms, two legs, two breasts, two ears and two eyes. It is just about possible to pick up two children at once, it is possible to breastfeed two babies, it is possible to cuddle two children on our laps or on each side of our body. But three? The ratio of babies to adults in nurseries is three babies to one adult? How can feeding, carrying and cuddling be achieved with this ratio?

Nature intended that babies should be brought up as the sole baby for at least nine months. This is achieved by ensuring that women do not give birth to another baby for at least nine months thus guaranteeing that the baby will have this precious individual time and attention. Yet everyday babies are placed in the care of adults who must provide for three babies at the same time. In some nurseries the baby room will cater for up to 15 babies each day!

Nature also intended that babies be brought up in a loving family, possibly with other siblings and extended family members.

Even in the large families that would have been seen 20 or 30 years ago it would have been normal to see gaps between children of one and two years. This natural environment enabled babies to watch, play and learn from older brothers and sisters as well as providing entertainment. Yet in nurseries, despite the evidence that it is good for children to grow and develop in mixed age ranges, we continue to confine children to strict age ranges within rooms. Why? Because this is easier for staff to manage, not because it is best for babies, toddlers or preschoolers.

Finally, and most importantly, nature designed humans to be born with the ability to become securely attached to a warm and nurturing care-giver. This attachment is crucial to the survival of the child in a number of ways. The bond of attachment prevents the toddling baby from straying far; it prevents the exploring child from going off with strangers and it supports the long term emotional health of our species. Historically, the mother has stayed at home to care for the child, therefore, the strongest bond of attachment is with her.

However, this attachment can just as easily be made with any warm and nurturing adult. The glue of this attachment is love, time and consistency of approach. Babies need one person with whom they can form a very secure attachment. When they have this then, and only then, can they really begin to play, learn, explore and discover the world and other people around them.

It may be difficult for the nursery to provide this consistency of care. Staff may work shifts or rotas that may mean that babies will have more than two different carers in one day and, perhaps, even more than that over the course of the week. Staff often find it difficult to cope with a baby who is clingy, fretful and demanding, though this is an absolutely natural and normal response to being left with a stranger.

We must understand the tremendous workload of staff as, under pressure, they may need to share their time with up to three babies, or four toddlers or, perhaps, as many as eight children aged three to five years at any one time. All of these children require an abundance of love, time and nurture as they learn to cope with nursery life. Many of the staff who care for babies in nursery have shared their concerns with me about not being able to meet the needs of the children. Adults tell me that they struggle to cope with the demands placed on them by these unrealistic ratios.

To summarise:

If you are returning to work then I urge you to read the next chapters of this book to help you to look at nurseries and choose the right one for your child.

Chapter Two

Deciding What To Do

'**What you should do is ....**' If you are a parent already, and even if you're not, you have probably heard this statement, normally issued by well-meaning friends and family prior to them telling you what you should do in your current situation. Friends will offer advice based on what they did or what they found useful to them, but they are not you and your child is not their child.

Rather than telling you what to do I want to offer you the opportunity to think through a couple of important areas for consideration. Friends and family who are using a private day nursery for their child will tell you how 'socialised' their child is. How he learned to share by the time he was just one year old! And better still how he knew all his 'colours, numbers, days of the week and shapes when he was just three years of age'. Beware of these parents as these are the same ones who will tell you, 'Oh my little Cruella was sleeping through the night when she was just seven weeks of age!'

Poor little Cruella didn't have a choice as mummy and daddy may have popped her into her cot and decided not to go to her when she cried so that she would 'learn' to sleep through.

Those parents who stayed at home to care for their little 'Montanna Moon-ray' will hold their heads up and tell you it was the, 'noblest sacrifice I have ever made, I gave up a career in accountancy to stay home and raise my own children'. Beware this may be the same parent who tells you that, little 'Montanna Moon-ray' refused to be weaned off the breast until finally daddy bribed him with a racing bike for his tenth birthday!

So let us consider some of the frequently asked questions or misconceptions people have about nursery care.

Nursery is good for children because............

Children need to be socialised and the best place for this will be in a nursery with other small children:

The truth:

Small children need company; this company can come from other adults and children of a variety of ages. Babies and small children love the company of other people; your baby will happily smile at the woman on the checkout at the local supermarket, the doctor, the dentist and anyone else who will take the time to smile and chat. Your baby needs lots of opportunities to practice essential communication skills and the place to do this is in an environment in which he or she will be heard; a place where there are a limited number of other voices clamouring for attention. Your baby also needs to meet and socialise with other adults and children whilst in the care of a person who loves him and who he feels safe with, that may be you, the father or another loving adult.

Children need to learn to share and take turns:

The truth:

Yes they do, but learning to share and take turns is related to their age, stage of development and their own experience. Children of only one or two years of age cannot share and take turns. Though some children will obey or comply with a parent's or adult's wish by giving up something they want simply because they have learnt to be compliant or the thing that had to be shared just wasn't that important to them.

Small children do not have the capacity to understand that other people have feelings too. From birth children are basically ego-centric, this means that their view of the world is centred on themselves, the world revolves around them. They are focused on and demand their needs to be met. This is how the human child survives. We cry to have our needs met and the available adult meets our need. Success!

Sometimes we adults expect children to do things that we would not do ourselves. We ask children to share their favourite toys, their time, their parents and sometimes even their bedrooms. But do you share your car, house, clothes, jewellery, husband or partner? Don't you have some possessions that are special to you, that you would rather not share? It is my belief that we ask of children that which we are not prepared to do ourselves. I think of this as a 'second class' attitude to childhood.

With help and at the right time and in the right situation a small child will begin to understand that by allowing another child to play with their toys the fun can be enjoyed by both children. But for some children this will not happen until they are four or five years of age..... and that's OK. Attendance at nursery is not directly linked to the ability to share. The small child can learn this lesson bit by bit with the help of a loving adult, in or out of nursery.

Nursery care is really expensive:

The truth:

The decision you make about the type of care you purchase for your child is one of the most important decisions you will make. The early years of a child's life lays the foundations for his future development in all areas of his life. The question should not be about cheap or expensive but should actually be about value. How much value do you place on where and how your child will spend their days? In every area of life, quality costs. This is just about how much you are willing to pay for the best.

Education begins at school, nursery is just for play:

The truth:

Babies' brains are largely undeveloped at birth. By the time the child is three years of age eighty percent of the brain is hard-wired. The experiences of the first three years impact upon the long-term growth and development of the child. Education begins from birth. Babies are sensory beings; they learn through the positive experiences of touch, taste, smell, sight and the sounds they encounter in their world. In order to learn from these experiences they must be repeated. The way in which the baby is repeatedly held, sang to, cuddled, fed and experiences familiar surroundings all provide security and help to lay down neural pathways in the brain. The brain is stimulated, growth and development occurs. This is true, also, of the negative experiences, being left to cry for too long, not being picked up when needed, being left hungry for too long. The baby learns from these experiences too. It is crucial that the nursery staff understand that these early years are important and that the role they have to play during the 'baby' years matters. Education begins from birth; from the first loving smile we receive from our mother or father we learn about our life.

Nurseries should plan experiences for babies which support all areas of their growth and development. Beware the nursery that tells you, children learn through play. Whilst this is true it is not an accurate description of what play should be.

Play is the work of the child and it is important that the child experiences a wide range of play opportunities. But play must be scaffolded by knowledgeable adults who know the child well. They must understand the child's stage of development and be able to support further learning and development by planning structured, well thought-out activities.

Children racing about a large outdoor space on bikes may, in my opinion, simply be experiencing what I term as 'hands-on/brains-off play' It's just a good old race around. That's OK for a very short period each day to run off all that energy, but that's not acceptable in high quality settings.

To summarise:

Having a child is part of the cycle of life, without **them** there is no **us**.

I have witnessed the experiences of children, demeaned to second class status, they spend their time in low quality nurseries with disenfranchised, poorly-paid adults. If we value our children we need to value the place and people they will spend their time with every day. We need to raise the child to first class citizenship every day. When choosing nursery ask, would I like to spend my day in this place and with these people every day?

To share our genes, our life, our knowledge, our interests and our time with another human being who is programmed to love us and want to be with us, to learn from us and to communicate with us is the greatest privilege of all time.

Don't believe me? Just ask the childless couple who invest all of their love, time, money and energy into trying to have a baby. Think too about the thousands of single people who long for someone to love and share their lives with. On finding that special 'someone' they will tell you how lucky they are, how blessed they were to find each other. It is not a sacrifice to spend time together, it is an investment in their future as they begin to share an interest in each other's life. There is no sacrifice, only joy and pleasure in each other's company.

So I say to every adult who works with children, to share, our life, our knowledge, our interests and our time with another human being who is programmed to love us and want to be with us, to learn from us and to communicate with us is the greatest privilege of all time.

Chapter 3

What To Look For

So you have made a decision to start looking at nurseries, you've seen a nice one in a convenient location near to where you live or work.

It is the kind of place with cute painted pictures on the windows and a pretty garden with lots of shiny plastic toys in the garden. But can you really tell by looking at the outside? Yes, but only if you know what you are looking for. So let's begin to gather some vital clues about the difference between a good nursery and a not-so-good one.

A word of caution here, this list will give you some of the important things to consider when choosing but you should also take note of what you instinctively feel.

Make an Appointment or Turn up Unannounced?

Both of these ways have their merits. Some nurseries believe that if they encourage you to turn up unannounced this will give you confidence that you can come at any time as they are always able to receive visitors. They don't put on a show. This is a good sign. However, I know some very good nurseries where they want you to make an appointment first just so the manager can schedule time to spend with you in her diary because they value you and will not want to run the risk of not being available. This too is a good sign.

My advice is to make an appointment so that you can spend time asking the manager important questions and then pop-in unannounced on a number of other occasions as you will then see the nursery across a range of times and activities. Do not make a decision until you have visited several times.

If you are told at any time that the nursery prefers you to ring before coming to collect your child early, settle him in or spend time with your child on whatever pretext then this may not a good sign.

The Outside of the Building:

What to look for:

The building should look neat and well-maintained. Windows with clean blinds or shutters or painted pictures are all OK. The nursery should have bright and clear signage with the nursery logo or name on it. The building should look as though it is cared for by a very house-proud owner. This is important because it tells you something about the business mentality of the owner. The owner who lives on-site, nearby or who also manages the business will know that first impressions count, they won't want to go to work every day to a shabby and run-down establishment.

Some of my clients are owners of several nurseries, some are business people and some live in other countries. Many of these people have other business interests, but are keenly interested in their nurseries. However, this is not always the case. I have worked with some nurseries where the owner, a successful builder, contractor or entrepreneur never goes near the nursery and spends little effort or capital investment in the place. Shabby paintwork, poorly maintained building and grounds as well as staff who appear to lack motivation and interest in their role may all point to a disinterested owner. A disinterested owner may hold the purse strings very tightly.

What you need to ask/know:

Who owns the building? How often do they visit it? Do they live on-site or nearby? Do they have other nurseries or businesses?

Beware of:

- Peeling paint, rotten woodwork, dirty windows and poor fencing.

- The nursery sign that looks as if it has been hanging from a thread since time began and is dirty or faded.

- Car park or play areas that appear uncared for with litter and debris left lying around.

- Hanging baskets that no longer have any sign of life; they were probably bought by a well-meaning manager with too little time or inclination to care for them.

Ease of Access to the Building/Outside Area:

What to look for:

This is important as you actually want it to be really quite difficult to get into the building, a bit like escaping from Alcatraz but in reverse. Why? Well if it is hard for you to get in as a prospective parent, then think how hard it would be for a stranger to get in and take a child or for a child to get out.

On arrival at the building you should not be able to get in at all, unless there is a small reception area which does not allow access to the main nursery. Normally there is a key-pad system for staff, a bell or an intercom system that you will need to use to draw attention to your arrival. If, however, you are waiting to gain entry or to make someone aware of your arrival and a passing parent or staff member simply opens the door to you before moving on their way, then this is not the place to leave your child. If this does happen please raise this with the nursery as a security issue. Do not be fobbed off with excuses such as, 'Oh that is our student/new staff, they don't know the routine yet'. They should have been inducted into the setting and should not be 'on the floor' until they are able to understand simple procedures such as not letting strangers into nurseries!

What should happen is that the door is opened by a member of staff who asks who you are, what your business is and asks you to sign in and wait there until someone comes for you. Use this opportunity to look around the entrance area. Do the doors have a double handle system which means that small children who find themselves in this area, with or without a parent, cannot open the doors to let themselves out?

Don't worry if you have to wait a little for the manager to show you around as nursery life is very busy and even if you have pre-booked a visit the unexpected can occur.

If the nursery has a car park area which is not also for the children's play, this should be clean and tidy with marked bays and directions to the entrance of the building.

What you need to know or ask:

What are the security arrangements for collecting my child? Who can collect them and how will you know that person if they have never been here before?

Security should be a well laid-down procedure that everyone adheres to. Check this out by asking what the procedure is then get a different member of staff to 'remind' you of the policy. If this differs from person to person it may indicate that a policy is in place but this has become relaxed after time.

The security arrangements should include either a key code for entry which is known by only two family members for each child or a password which is known by staff and can be given to anyone with permission to collect the child in one-off situations. The password may change each time it is used.

Whatever procedures the nursery employs they should remain rigorous and in place throughout the time your child attends.

Beware if:

- You are told, 'Just tell us each day when you drop off who is to collect your child and that's OK'.

The Garden or Play Area:

This is an important area. If you are considering using a nursery on a full-time basis then this will be the main outside play experience your child has.

The play area should be large enough to cater for the numbers of children who attend the nursery on a daily basis. However each room, or group, may need to take turns using the outside space. Incredibly, it has only recently been understood that it is absolutely paramount that all children access the outdoors several times each day whatever the weather.

For more information about the values of outside play spaces it is worth looking at the excellent work of organisations such as, Learning through Landscapes and Forest Schools. The web address for both of these is in the 'Further Information' section at the end of this book.

It is just as important that children get out of the nursery and into the community on a regular basis. This is because the wider community forms a large part of a child's experience; allowing the child to learn about other people and to feel a sense of belonging as they visit the shops, parks and facilities of the area in which they live.

Consider, if you will, what it would be like if your view of the world was based solely on the associations you have with the people you work with! Frightening isn't it? You probably cope with the people in your work life either because you're extremely lucky and have found a truly lovely bunch of well-rounded and wonderful, caring people. Or because you know that your time each day with them is limited and although some of them are complete pains you know lots of people who aren't. You have also learned skills to help you cope. Your child needs a whole view of the world that goes beyond the confines of the nursery staff and playground.

Unfortunately some nurseries that have been converted for use and in existence for many years may have very inadequate outdoor play spaces.

The best nurseries will have an ethos that values outdoor play and this will be evident in both resources and staff attitudes. You may be asked to supply your child with wellingtons and all-weather gear. You may be told that it is a good idea not to dress your child in good clothes as they will get very messy and dirty. You will need to provide a change of dry clothes. You may also be told that children will go outside even if they have a slight cold or runny nose. All of these are good signs.

Germs spread like wild-fire in warm rooms. Getting the children out-of-doors will provide them with an opportunity to run off excess energy, build a healthy appetite, aid restful sleep and provide them with healthy fresh air.

What to Look for:

Areas with green landscaping such as bushes, trees and grass. Look for areas where children can experience digging, planting and growing. Look for opportunities for children to be able to play quietly without being mown down by wheeled toys.

Look for den-making areas and opportunities for children to paint, draw and colour on a large scale. Look for spaces where children can use large construction materials such as crates, planks, pipes and logs.

Check that the outdoor space is fitted with good, high fencing to protect the property from vandalism and lockable safe storage where everything is neatly stored.

The area should appear swept and cleaned with toys and resources looking clean and well-cared for.

Look for nursery rooms with doors that lead immediately to the outdoor play space.

What you need to know or ask:

How often will your child get outside every day? Is the area shared with other groups? How do staff who have to care for non-mobile babies or toddlers ensure that they get outside every day? If there is a door from each room into the play area, is this kept open and are children allowed free access to the outdoor space? Is there a designated area for babies so that they are able to sit and play without being mown down? How long are the children outside? How often do children go out into the surrounding area? Are trips and visits to local attractions planned? Are children able to play out all year long? Are outdoor activities planned or are they purely spontaneous?

Beware of:

- Large areas of tarmac with an abundance of shiny plastic toys and wheeled vehicles.

- A lack of order or organisation in the play area and staff who stand around like prison warders chatting in groups or to one another.

- Staff who tell you, 'Yes we get out all the time when the weather is nice'.

- Nurseries where children go out once or twice a day for about fifteen minutes, 'If the weather is OK'.

- Very small play areas for a large number of children.

- Toddler rooms on the first floor; with the best will in the world this will make going out to play very difficult and staff need to organise it like a military procedure. This may deter the less enthusiastic staff member from taking her children out.

Chapter 4

The Show-Around

What to look for:

It is probably better to look around the nursery before sitting down to chat with the manager. In this way you can make a mental, or a written note, of anything you see that you would like to ask questions about.

If you have dropped in unannounced then you may expect to be shown around by a member of staff, but not necessarily the manager. This is fine but you should then make an appointment of least an hour to talk through policies, contracts and questions with the manager. Do not be tempted to sign any sort of agreement on your first visit.

At this first visit insist on seeing all of the nursery and not just the room that your child will first attend. You may also have an opportunity to meet with a member of staff that will be appointed as your child's 'key person'*. If this doesn't happen, don't worry it is quite normal for this to happen later.

It is perfectly acceptable to ask for a second or third look around so that you can get a clearer picture of the other rooms your child will move on to. I have known some nurseries where there is a good deal of time, money and effort spent on making the 'baby room' very appealing as this is the room first seen and used by new parents. When looking around make sure you see the kitchen. This is important as this can tell you much about the food your child will be given and the general health and hygiene of the nursery.

OK, let's go. Remember this is what you may look for at the first look around. I will give a more detailed account of each room later. For now, see how many of these you can see.

Walls, Doors and Windows:

You are looking for walls that are clean, painted and well-maintained. Peeling paint, or plaster, old, over-painted wood-chip wallpaper are not good signs.

Many nurseries paint the walls in the most luminous and garish colour as if this is what they think children like. I have not seen any research that suggests this is the case. However, it is not a black mark against them if this is how the nursery is decorated. You should see nice, well-cared for displays of children's work and lots of photographs of children at play.

The doors should open and close easily and may have double handles to prevent children leaving the building, which may not be necessary if it is impossible to get past the reception area. If there is a door which leads immediately to the outdoor play area in each room this is great. Is it open? Today it is good practice to have, where possible, a door that leads to the outdoor area which is kept open so that children may freely choose to play out-of-doors.

The windows should be clean and well-maintained so that they can be opened for ventilation. Most nurseries do not have windows that small children can look out of.

It seems, even when buildings are purposely designed for small children, we forget the most important fact. They are small so they need windows that reach to the ground, or windows that are at least placed lower down in the wall! Small children need to be able to see out of the window to see the weather, people passing-by, the traffic or nature in the landscape.

Are the window sills used to display books or toys, are they clean and tidy or is there a motley collection of the lost or broken toys and work products of the staff? Whether you prefer the windows to be painted with pictures or if they have blinds really is just a matter of choice. Ask yourself, 'Could I spend the next 12, 18 or 24 months, five days a week in a room like this? How would it make me feel?

Floors:

The ideal arrangement in a nursery room is to have about half of the room carpeted and half of it in a hard-wearing and washable surface. Some nurseries have washable floor covering throughout and provide soft carpeting by using rugs. This is absolutely fine. What you want to check out is that the floors are clean. Are they swept and mopped if needed after lunch? Do toys litter the floor long after children have finished playing with them? Does the carpet have worn patches, look dirty and stained? Take a minute to look at the carpeted areas and ask would I like to sit on them every day?

Tables, Chairs and Furniture:

The tables should be clean and well-maintained, they may be wood or laminated tops. The tables may be used for both messy activities and for serving and eating meals so they must be scrupulously clean, though they may be stained over a period of time.

The bookcases and shelving units should look in good order and should not look as if they are about to fall down or topple over. Cupboards and shelves should display an arrangement of toys which are neatly labelled and tidy.

Shelving units which display a range of odd toys and games in no particular order or are used to house odd toys and work products of staff may demonstrate a lack of organisation in the room.

All nursery rooms will need to have enough chairs for every child to sit for meals. These can sometimes take up valuable play space so many nurseries just stack these out of the way until needed. Check that these do not block fire doors or cause a hazard to small toddlers who are learning to walk and climb!

Toys and Resources:

An abundance of shiny plastic toys is definitely no reason to choose one nursery over another. Remember it is the presence of a loving adult that will make the playing with toys (even a cardboard box) a valuable experience.

You should look for a wide range of toys and equipment for all types of play. I cover this in much more detail later. For now look to see if toys include both wooden and plastic types. If there are toys for floor play and toys for table-top play, are they neatly organised in labelled boxes so that children can help themselves?

Are there messy play activities too and aprons for children to wear?

Don't worry if it all looks a little messy and untidy when children are playing; is there a general air of happy-busy play or are you witnessing chaos on a grand scale?

Staff:

Do staff smile and say, 'Hello' when you come into the room? Don't expect them to stop what they are doing as they are paid to work with the children so you wouldn't really want them to abandon their post. Is there a general feeling of calm or are staff shouting above the din to make themselves heard?

Do staff sit around at the table with children but are not really chatting to them or joining in their play. Do staff sit together rather than with the children?

Do staff look clean, tidy, awake, presentable, energetic, lively and fun? Or do they look like they have just fallen out of bed and are dealing with a huge hangover, (I've seen all of this so I am serious)?

Does the nursery have a mixed staff team in which there are males as well as females and both young and mature staff?

Is the nursery team mainly made up of very young staff who do not have children of their own? This is important on several levels because different ages bring different experiences to the nursery. More mature staff who have had their own children may be more patient and more loving, providing lots of cuddles and hugs. Younger staff may be more 'fun', caring less about the mess and be much more willing to engage children in big, messy, creative play experiences. Males are always popular in nurseries with all the children. We need more males working in nurseries and schools. We could discuss at length why this is but this is not the time to talk about the dramatic changes in society and the subsequent effects on the lives of children (I'll save that for another book).

There are still too few males in day care, but the numbers are growing. They seem to bring a more physical type of play for the children, engaging them in running, climbing and sporting activities.

You may be concerned if you see staff 'corral' children onto the carpeted area and keep them sitting still for long periods of time prior to lunch, snack, home-time or whilst they tidy up. Small children have a very short attention span; you may keep them engaged watching or listening to something for maybe just a minute or two for each year of age. However, they will happily play for much longer when they are actively involved.

Children:

Do the children seem happy? Are there a number of them crying loudly?

Crying children is, unfortunately, part of nursery life but what you should not see is a child, or worse still, children wandering around the room crying alone. They should not be sitting in cots, highchairs or bouncing seats crying without adult attention. This is not acceptable.

Let me clarify this. It is impossible to pick a baby up every time he cries in nursery because the practitioner will have three babies to care for and a multitude of tasks to be accomplished. But what the adult (parent or staff) should do is to acknowledge the child's cries. 'I know you're hungry, I'm getting your bottle', 'I'm only here, I'm coming now'. You may wonder what difference this makes to the child as they can't understand what's being said. Well they may not understand the words but they will understand that when they cry the adult responds with warmth and empathy and they will feel comforted by this.

A child who is crying, even loudly, but is being comforted by an adult is an acceptable face of nursery life.

Safety:

Fire drills are an important part of nursery procedures which must be carried out regularly. There is no definitive guide about how often these procedures should be practiced, but good settings will hold a fire drill whenever new staff join the team or at least every other month. The fire drill should be held at different times of the day so that all staff know what to do at any given time in an emergency.

It is particularly important that drills are practiced, when you consider that a practitioner may have to evacuate up to three babies safely and swiftly on her own. You may want to ask the setting what arrangements are made for the evacuation of immobile babies and toddlers, when the last fire drill was and what date is the next one? You may ask how long it took to evacuate all children at the last fire drill? All settings must keep accurate records of fire drill procedures so they should be able to retrieve this information for you.

First Aid:

The statutory guidance states that, 'at least one person with a current paediatric first aid qualification must be on the premises when children are present'. In a large building or setting with many rooms this is insufficient. In good or high quality settings all staff will hold a paediatric first aid qualification.

Comfort:

The statutory guidance regarding room temperatures and ventilation requires settings to ensure that all rooms where children are cared for are well-ventilated and have windows that can be opened safely to allow for the free-flow of air. This is particularly important when considering the arrangements for sleeping infants. Practitioners should be able to quickly and easily reduce or increase the temperature of the room if needed.

The Kitchen:

There is no reason for you not to be able to see the kitchen. However, it is quite understandable if you are asked to see this another time if your visit coincides with the serving up or delivery of meals.

You want to see a kitchen that is clean, hygienic, organised and well- maintained.

You should also see kitchen staff who are dressed in appropriate clothes and wearing 'chef's whites' or an apron. Other staff may go into the kitchen to collect food but should not be involved in the preparation of food unless they are wearing an apron.

High quality nurseries will understand the value of children being able to cook and help to prepare food. Can children enter the kitchen, do they know the chef? Are there opportunities for children to help?

No one is allowed to smoke in the kitchen or anywhere else in the nursery. In fact in a high quality nursery the staff will not be allowed to come to work in any clothes that they may smoke in. The kitchen should have a notice board with routines, guidelines and procedures for maintaining a healthy and safe kitchen.

Settings serving or preparing food for children must register with the local authority environmental health department to do so. The person preparing or serving food must be suitably qualified. They should hold a Level 2 Food Handlers certificate as a minimum requirement. The Food Standards Agency (FSA) now requires local authorities to inspect premises where food is being prepared or served and provide a food hygiene rate. This rate should be clearly displayed in the setting. If this is not evident ask the setting about their rate. Rating is from 0-5 with 5 being the highest score. Ideally the setting will have a 4 or 5, anything below this is not acceptable.

On 13 December 2014, new legislation (the EU Food Information for Consumers Regulation No. 1169/2011) came into force which requires food businesses to provide allergy information on food being sold, prepared and served. In practice this means that the chef in the nursery will hold detailed information about the possible allergens in all food products whether they are bought in or made on the premises. The FSA provide on-line training for chefs and good settings will ensure that chefs are well trained and compliant with the regulations.

Here is the tick list that you may want to use on your visit to the nursery.

The Tick List

Area Seen	Yes	No
Walls, Doors and Windows: Clean, tidy and well-maintained?		
Floors: Carpet and washable flooring both clean and well-maintained?		
Tables, Chairs and Furniture: Clean and well-maintained, stacked or arranged safely?		
Toys and Resources: A good mix of wooden, natural and plastic? All clean, organised and sufficient for numbers and age of children?		

Staff: Clean, friendly and mixed age ranges and qualifications? Playing with children?		
Children: Happy, active and playing?		
Kitchen: Clean, safe and hygienic? Staff wearing appropriate clothes/uniform? Children can access the space to cook, help or eat?		

Chapter 5

Meeting the Manager

Let's think for a moment about what you may reasonably expect the manager to be like and the role she holds. The best way for me to do this is to tell you what is expected of a person who holds a management post. As I have indicated, just for ease I shall use the term 'she' in reference to the manager, however, we may agree that this position can just as easily be held by a man as a woman. That said, I have not yet come across a male manager in a day nursery.

The manager should be smart, clean and well-dressed. Does that seem obvious? Well it may to you, but I have seen many managers who regularly turn up for work in jeans, trainers, tracksuit bottoms, a sloppy tee-shirt and greasy dragged-back-into-a-pony-tail hair. Now you may think that this really shouldn't matter if she is good at her job.

I see it like this; anyone who isn't organised enough each morning to have a wash, do her hair and find something clean, tidy and well-pressed to wear even before she gets to work does not inspire confidence in me. How are they going to organise and manage a working nursery and its' staff? The nursery manager's job is extremely busy, she will hit the ground running almost every day of the week. She must be prepared for the challenges, decisions and meetings she will have. She is the ambassador of the business for the owner and must inspire complete confidence in the parents who entrust their children to her care.

The manager must have a Child Care Qualification at Level 3.

Most good managers will also have a Level 4 or 5 qualification, which may be in either management or a childcare related field. The manager may work with an owner or for an owner of a nursery. The owner may also be the manager if they are suitably qualified.

The manager will be responsible for overseeing all aspects of nursery life. She will manage staff, liaise with the local authority sure start team responsible for the quality and assurance at the nursery (different authorities have different titles for this team). These are professionals who offer advice and guidance to nurseries, in their area, in relation to the care and education of children.

The manager will oversee the delivery of the care and education of all children and will oversee the care of children with Special Educational Needs (SEN). She will work with other professionals outside of the nursery in promoting and managing the needs of the children. The manager will also be responsible for collecting fees and managing budgets. She will take the lead role in 'safeguarding' children. The nursery will also have a deputy manager who will assist the manager in her role, but is normally given particular areas of responsibility, such as SEN Coordinator. To fully support the manager, the deputy should be given some non-contact time. In large nurseries both the manager and the deputy will be supernumerary (not counted in the numbers of adults available to work with the children) in smaller nurseries it may be that the deputy has just one or two supernumerary days each week. This is absolutely fine. What is not so good is when the deputy's role is one in which she is never free to spend time in the office to learn the role of manager or to support the manager, or one in which she is the general 'dogsbody' doing the shopping, school-run, covering for the cook and any other person who doesn't turn up for work. This may happen occasionally to the owner, manager or deputy but should not be the norm.

The Contract:

All nurseries will have a contract for you to sign. This is normally non-negotiable and most of the nurseries I know enforce this to the letter, particularly in respect of fees. It is quite normal practice for a nursery to exclude a child from the nursery if the fees are late by as little as one week. Remember the nursery is a business and all nurseries are very likely to resort to legal action for late payment of fees.

Please do not be tempted to sign the contract at the first meeting; it is very important that you feel really happy that this is the right place for your child. If it is not already in the contract you may want to ask if they will allow you to have a one month agreement initially. This means that after the settling-in period you will have one month in which you can see if this is the right place for you and your child.

What you should ask or know:

Ask at the first meeting if you can have a copy of the contract to take home and look at carefully and to compare. This will show the nursery that you are serious and that you are looking at other nurseries.

Beware if:

They ask you to sign it on your first visit. Why are they so keen?

To summarise:

How well presented and maintained the outside of the building is may be a clue to how the business is managed.

The area that is allocated for children to play in is of vital importance to the health and well-being of your child.

If the nursery is hard to get into then it will be hard for a child to get out of.

If the first visit is a quick pop-in then make an appointment for a longer visit.

The manager is the captain of this ship, does she look, sound and act like she can navigate on a stormy day?

Take your time to study the contract as it is a legally binding document.

Chapter 6

Important Questions to Ask

The manager will have responsibility for ensuring that all of the policies and procedures of the setting are adhered to and carried out. In respect of policies, what you may find, and is most common, is that there are a large stack of files in the main office which contain the numerous, weighty and extremely long policy documents. The manager's job is ensuring that these are understood and implemented by all staff and that there are regular specific procedures in place to guarantee this.

What often happens is that policies are in place (large stack of files in the office) but in reality staff have only a vague idea about what to do in particular situations, or worse still, staff interpret the policies, in lieu of any real guidance, for themselves.

You should be given a prospectus which details all the policies and which gives a summarised version of each. In this chapter I have drawn up a set of questions that relate to the policies which are important to you which you may want to discuss with the manager when you meet. Don't be afraid of asking too many questions. This is a most important decision for your child's future and you need to get it right.

Question 1: What are the levels of qualifications of the staff throughout the nursery?

The nursery is allowed to have 50 percent of staff unqualified in any room. In each room there must be one Level 3 member of staff. Children cannot be left in the sole care of any member of staff who does not hold a Level 3 qualification.

Good nurseries tend to employ only qualified staff or those working towards a qualification.

Question 2: What numbers of staff are working towards or have a higher qualification?

Although this is not yet a requirement, it is good practice as every private day nursery will be required to employ a graduate who will take the lead role in overseeing the care and education for every child. Good nurseries are preparing for this now by supporting staff to undertake the relevant training. Much of this training will be out of nursery hours, but if your child's nursery needs to close occasionally for staff development then please support the nursery and staff. Much of the training for nursery staff is in staff's own time and they are frequently underpaid.

Where there are a number of staff involved in gaining additional qualifications this shows that the nursery is dedicated to maintaining high standards and that some staff are motivated.

Question 3: What is the turnover of staff like? How many have left in the last 12 months?

If the number of staff leaving is high you might want to think carefully about why this is. Are there too few incentives, are pay/conditions poor? Do they feel undervalued?

Happy staff will generally only leave as they climb the ladder or improve their qualifications; this is natural, but if they are leaving for other reasons there may be underlying problems within the team or management structure.

Occasionally when a nursery has been taken over by a new owner or manager then it is often the case that people will leave; this is more often a positive sign as a 'new broom sweeps clean'.

Question 4: Do you have regular staff meetings?

The normal procedure is to have meetings at least once each month for about an hour. Some nurseries will also have room meetings, these are held for about half-an-hour prior to the staff meetings. These are all positive signs showing that the nursery is interested in providing valuable opportunities for staff to get together with the management team and to feedback any issues or concerns before these get out of hand. Regular meetings are vital to the smooth-running of the nursery in respect of planning and team working. Don't be fobbed off with comments such as, 'No we don't like to bother staff by keeping them behind', 'The managers have a meeting and then feedback to staff later' or, 'No we think staff work hard enough during the day without keeping them back'. Other comments may include, 'Well we are such a small team that we don't need to meet after work as we are here all the time so we just chat stuff through as we go'.

High quality nurseries understand the importance of team meetings and remunerate staff for their time and build meetings and administrative duties into the weekly schedule.

Question 5: How do you manage to maintain the staff ratios and cover lunches, breaks and staff absence?

This is an area that can be quite difficult for nurseries to manage, and the answer given will tell you a lot about the nursery.

Let's first look at the ratios. This is the number of children each adult can care for according to the ages of the children as laid down by Ofsted. Remember that the people caring for your child are not super-human. Their qualification does not equip them with extra hands, eyes or feet. It provides them with additional knowledge which enables them to use or refine the skills needed to care for groups of small children. They are just ordinary people like you and I.

The ratios are:

- **one adult to every three babies and children under two years of age.**
- **one adult to every four children two to three years of age.**
- **one adult to every eight children three to five years of age, unless there is a qualified**

teacher, in which case she may have 13 children.

High quality nurseries may work below these ratios, thereby, ensuring that each child has a greater opportunity to fulfil his/her potential. Of course there are cost implications to this way of working.

This is not quite as simple as it appears because the nursery must also take into account the qualifications of each adult. However, on a daily basis and as a rough guide you should not leave your child in the care of any adult who does not hold a relevant qualification or an adult who has more children than she is allowed to care for.

The adult is allowed to care for more children when the children are asleep. So for example if there are five babies and two staff in the nursery room and at least two of the babies are asleep then it is acceptable for one member of staff to go for lunch. However, there would then be problem if one of the babies awoke and the remaining member of staff had four children awake and no one free to call on.

Many nurseries manage by moving staff around as children sleep and by using the manager to cover staff lunches. This is a little ad-hoc and can mean a chaotic and disorganised approach to lunch-time arrangements, which leads to staff feeling undervalued and frustrated, as well as lunch-breaks sometimes being cut short. It also means that small children will have a range of different adults bobbing in and out of the room to cover breaks and lunches. Good nurseries will either employ a small number of staff who work just to cover the lunch-time or will carry an extra one or two staff who are 'floaters' moving about the nursery to cover staff breaks, lunches and sickness.

Question 6: What opportunities are there for chatting to staff about my child's development?

The nursery should make provision for you to receive regular verbal feedback every day from your child's key person.

If your child is under three years of age this should be done as a written account in the form of a simple daily diary account of what your child has had to eat, how long they slept and if they had soiled or wet nappies. This is very important information, in the event that your child becomes ill overnight you would then have a written record to check on unusual sleep patterns, new foods eaten and bladder and bowel movements.

A written record is not normally done for the over-threes as they are much more able to communicate this information. The nursery normally has a menu on the wall to tell you what was offered each day to the children.

Good nurseries hold regular Parents Evenings for all parents. This may range from between once a year to once per term.

If you are told, 'We don't hold parents evenings because we find we are able to chat through things at the beginning and the end of the day', this is not good enough. You will want to have the opportunity to look through the records staff keep about your child's development and chat in private to your child's key person.

Question 7: Can I pop in anytime to see my baby?

All I want to say is if the answer is not, 'Yes of course' then run. Good nurseries want to work with parents; they welcome them. Never leave your child at a nursery where you can't get across the threshold anytime you want or need. There is no valid reason for disallowing parent's access. I have heard many excuses from nurseries such as, 'It is a security issue, we don't like having parents wandering about' or, 'It upsets the other children when they see parents collecting their children'. Do not be fobbed off with any excuse at all!

Question 8: What sort of menu is offered?

The nursery should be able to provide you with a menu plan which will probably work on a four week rota. This should have a balance of fresh vegetables, (not tinned), fresh fruit as well as fresh meat and fish. You can expect your child to have a very healthy diet today in nurseries as more and more local authorities work with nurseries to promote healthy eating. Children will normally be offered a two course lunch. The main course will normally be some sort of fish, meat or vegetable 'bake' or casserole with one or two vegetables offered for choice. Chips should feature no more than once each week, if at all, and never for babies. There should not be too many sweet desserts following the main course. It is normal to have cake and custard, rice pudding or ice cream type desserts just once or twice each week. The rest of the time children may be offered yoghurt, fresh fruit or cheese and crackers after the main course.

Children will also be offered an early morning snack which, again, should be healthy. Beware of nurseries that offer toast or biscuits with juice every day. Children should be offered fresh water and milk only throughout the day. Toast is good but only if this is good quality brown bread with a little spread. This should not be offered every day.

Children will be given a light tea at about 3pm. This is not supposed to replace an evening meal but will just keep children going until they get home.

Some older children will need a full meal on arriving home others will need just another light meal before bed. The tea will normally be a small portion of beans-on-toast, crumpets, cheese and crackers or a sandwich. This is normally just one course with water or milk.

You should be told that the nursery can cater for religious food preferences, as well as vegetarian or vegan diets and will, of course, be able to cater for children with allergies.

If your child is a baby you should expect to supply the breast or formula milk your child needs. This will either need to be ready-made into bottles or the nursery will do this for you. You may want to provide your own home-made pureéd food for your baby to eat and this is perfectly acceptable.

Question 9: What do I need to bring for my child?

You should expect to provide your child with a bag in which you can put a change of clothes and underwear, if your child is toilet trained, or nappies, nappy cream and wipes. Most nurseries will expect you to provide sun-block and hat as well as wet-weather clothes and footwear. You may also include any small item your child needs as a comforter such as a dummy or teddy bear.

If the nursery provides nappies, wipes and/or wet weather clothes this is a big bonus.

You should not be told that your child cannot have his dummy or comforter in nursery but both you and the staff will want to work together so that your child can keep his dummy purely for nap-times. Children who keep their dummies in throughout the day have their ability to communicate seriously hindered. After all one of the most effective ways of communicating our feelings is to verbalise them.

How can we expect children to be good communicators if in effect we 'plug' the very best tool for the job?

To summarise:

The answers to the questions you ask are important, they tell you about the nursery and the care that the nursery is able to provide for your child.

Do not be afraid to ask as many questions as you need and don't be afraid to walk away.

You may also find it useful to take another person with you to look around.

Overleaf I have listed the questions again but this time with a space beneath each one for you to record the answers if you so wish.

Question 1: What are the levels of qualifications of the staff throughout the nursery?

Question 2: What numbers of staff are working towards or have a higher qualification?

Question 3: What is the turnover of staff like? How many have left in the last 12 months?

Question 4: Do you have regular staff meetings?

Question 5: How do you manage to maintain the staff ratios and cover lunches, breaks and staff absence?

Question 6: What opportunities are there for chatting to staff about my child's development?

Question 7: Can I pop in anytime to see my baby/child?

Question 8: What sort of menu is offered?

Question 9: What do I need to bring for my child?

Chapter 7

The Settling-in Period

I am going to devote some time to discussing this point as it is one of the most singularly important factors in helping your child to settle properly into the nursery and to become attached to another person. It is also the area that some nursery staff complain about; they feel that some parents do not devote sufficient time to the process of settling the child in.

I believe this is simply because parents don't know how crucial the settling-in period is. If your child is already happily settled in nursery then feel free to skip this chapter, although reading this may also provide you with useful information about why some children behave and react the way they do.

The settling-in period is exactly that. It provides opportunities for you to visit the nursery with your child to help him to become acclimatised. You should not be expected to pay for the settling-in period. You would normally be expected to stay with your child for the first few visits, then leave him for very short periods of time in the care of one of the staff. The time that you leave your child grows longer over each visit. However, in many nurseries this is a process that is curtailed either because the parent has not understood the value of the process or because they have left insufficient time for this before they need to resume their employment. In some circumstances the nursery also does not understand the long-term benefits of a long settling-in process. The settling-in period should be a time when your child can become familiar with the surroundings, smell, sounds and faces of new people. But it is also so an opportunity for staff to learn about your child from the person who knows him best of all, and that is you.

This process is not different for a child of three months or three years. The same commitment to time should be given to each child. Parents will sometimes spend more time settling the two or three year old in because at this age the child is much more likely to make their feelings known by crying, shouting and screaming.

When a baby is very small, under nine months of age, they can often be left with anyone at all without protesting. Mothers will often complain that they miss the baby more than the baby misses them! There is a reason for this. When we are small we are unable to keep a picture in our head of either people or objects.

Jean Piaget, Child Cognitivist and Theorist, describes the stage of development, when a child can keep a picture or image, of the person they are attached to, in their head as 'Person Permanence'. This will happen sometime between seven and nine months of age. Around this age you may find that one week you can happily drop little 'Sigourney' off at Grandma's without protest and the next week she bellows loud enough to win a gold medal in the Baby-Bellowing Competition at the shopping centre.

Because a very young baby will allow themselves to be handed over from one person to another or does not cry loudly on being left does not mean that they are happily settled. Yet some nurseries and parents cut short the settling-in period because the child appears to be OK.

Your child has just spent the whole of his life so far being cared for by one or two special people who do things for him exactly as they should be done.

It will have taken some time for you to get to know exactly what each of your child's different cries mean. Consider how long it was before you were able to distinguish between a cry that was one of either pain, fear, hunger, tiredness or just a 'need-a-cuddle' cry?

A baby's cry is one of their most effective methods of communication, they are born with just one type of cry, but over, time the baby learns to cry in different ways for different things.

The role of the adult is to learn, as quickly as possible, to discern the meaning behind each of these cries and to respond to meet the need. If we did not respond to the cries of the baby, then the baby would not survive. You and your baby will learn together about each other. The baby will cry for food and you will respond by offering the breast or bottle and your baby will be comforted. What is important here is to state clearly that babies do not cry for no reason at all. Babies cry in response to a need. They are totally unable to predict that you will pick them up if they cry. They do not cry because they want you to pick them up, they cry because they need comfort of a type.

Eventually by the time your child is about 12 months of age they will learn that when they cry they can rely on you to meet their needs. They will, in turn, learn to trust you.

If your baby is less than nine months of age when you take them to nursery it is crucial that the person you leave them with has had a long period of time to get to know your child's likes, needs and wants. This new person now needs to learn to accurately interpret the cries of your child. When he is left in the care of a relative stranger his world may be thrown upside down as he cries to have his needs met but now this person carries out routines in a totally different way.

Earlier on I discussed how children learn about the world and other people from a base of secure relationships. Now your child needs to learn about his key person whilst he is safely in your care. Bit by bit, and over time you can teach the key person to interpret your baby's cries, body language and gestures.

Bit by bit your baby will become familiar with the room, furniture, sounds and the other adult because you are with him giving him the security to explore new places and people. All of this takes time, but it is a long-term investment in the emotional independence and security of your child. There are no short cuts. I have seen too many children in nurseries who are insecure, they crave the attention of adults and this is evidenced in either their poor behaviour (biting, fighting, kicking and pinching others) or by allowing themselves to be passed from adult to adult without complaint.

The other obvious advantage of spending lots of time settling your child into the nursery is that you are much more likely to get a real taste of what the nursery is like.

Are staff able to cope with the demands of small children? Do they complain about other staff in front of children? Do they favour some children more than others?

Are they organised and provide a range of exciting activities for children? Do they respond quickly to the needs of babies, moving them one place to another, talking to them gently, and importantly, holding them to feed them by bottle?

High quality settings will place no constraints upon you to settle your child quickly and may even offer you stay and play or drop-in sessions weekly and without charge.

You've settled him in but he still cries!

OK, but what if you have been through whole process and your child still cries when you leave him?

If you know you spent a long time settling him in and helping him get used to nursery life then you must ask why he is still unhappy when you go?

Worst case scenario is that the nursery has some staff that really are not very nice people, there are things that happen during the nursery day that make your child unhappy and your child is not attached to his key person. This does happen and children are very sensitive to the emotions and feelings they pick up from other people. If you suspect that this is the case then you may want to move your child to another nursery or to a childminder. I have known parents who have done this and have been very happy that they did. Although you will need to go through the settling-in process again it will be worth it when every time you pick your child up and he is happy and settled and every morning when he 'bounces' into nursery to see his 'friends'.

But what if you like your child's key person, are you completely happy that this person is a nice, good kind and reliable person? OK, does your child feel the same? Does he look comforted and happy with his key person? If the answer is yes, then work with her to hand your child over in a way which you can cope with, try to make sure that you always hand him over to the same person each day and that should, of course, be his key person. You may be told that, 'He is fine as soon as you've gone, just go' and this may be true. You need to check out this claim. If they have CCTV you can check this way. If not, you may need to stand in the reception area for a while then creep along to the room and look in on him unseen. If he really does stop crying as soon as you have gone then it may be that your child is sensitive to your feelings about handing him over and leaving him. It can happen that your child begins to sense your feelings of unease as you leave him. It is important to be able to interpret your child's cries in this situation too. Is your child protesting at being left? The chances are that if he settles quickly and happily as soon as you have gone then this is protest. After all the very best situation for your child is to have a devoted parent providing individual care 24 hours a day. Cries of protest are natural and will be loud, but short-lived. If your child continues to cry throughout the day, is miserable and hard to console, you should reconsider your options.

The best way to deal with cries of protest then is to be as matter of fact as you can.

Get your child ready for nursery and try to remain calm and in control. Some children will begin to cry even before they arrive at nursery. Don't be tempted to shout at your child or tell him he is naughty or silly; his feelings are real and they matter. Do not lie to him and pretend you are going somewhere else, your child needs to trust you and know that even when it is an unpleasant situation you are always truthful. Acknowledge your child's feelings, 'I know you're upset, but you will be fine, Mary will look after you and I know you will have a lovely time'. On arriving at the room with your child hand him over to his key person, give your child a quick kiss and leave. Never ever sneak off without saying goodbye. Many parents will stay for a little while because the child has begun to cry and, as soon as he is happily, playing sneak out. This can make a child feel very insecure. How does he know that the next time he is happily playing at home you are not going to sneak out?

Do not tell him that you are just popping to the car, shops etc., but will be back in a minute. It is a lie, and your child may spend the rest of the day waiting for you. It will not help him learn to understand time or to manage time or his feelings later on.

Give your child a 'picture' of when you will return, 'Mummy is going to work but I will be back after you have had your tea in nursery'.

Good nursery staff will use a pictorial timetable to help children to understand the passage of time and the routines of the day.

The settling-in period is also about you learning to trust your child's key person so that together you can best support your child and meet his needs.

To summarise:

The settling-in period can begin as soon as you decide to use a nursery.

You do not normally pay for any short sessions you have during the settling-in period.

You can accompany your child as often as you like without paying during this period.

Beware of nurseries that encourage a very short settling-in period or want you to drop a child at the door.

Chapter 8

The Key Person Role

The key person role is now mostly understood by all nurseries and staff. The role is not new; Margaret Macmillan, one of the first people in England to provide day care for children under five in the 1900's called this way of caring for a small number of children, the 'Care Working' system.

A key person is an adult who will take responsibility for particular areas of care for a small number of children. Their aim is to build a bond of attachment with each of their 'key children' it is important that your child is attached to his key person. This bond of attachment keeps a child safe, allowing them to explore their environment and other people from a base of secure relationships.

The key person will take responsibility for all of the intimate care routines. This will include, nappy-changes, feeding by bottle or spoon, comforting a child who is upset and perhaps putting them down for their nap or getting them up. There will be other duties such as maintaining the child's development records and learning journey as well as planning activities for key children. The key person will also work hand-in-hand with the parents to provide consistency of approach. She should be friendly and approachable, but not a friend. All children in nursery will be appointed a key person. The role changes as children are able to do more for themselves, but each child should have someone who takes particular care of them. The key person is someone to whom you can go to discuss areas of concern.

However, this way of working is difficult for nurseries to implement as staff don't work the same number of hours that children attend nursery. Indeed it is fair to say that some children will attend nursery for more hours than any member of staff, therefore, your child will not always have their key person available to them.

This is, in fact, one of the reasons why many parents prefer to use a childminder.

He or she is always available to the child, opening the door to the first child and still available to the last.

Most nurseries, in this situation, appoint a 'back-up key person', another adult the child is familiar with. This is a person who is in the same room as the child and who is available when the key person is not.

The important point to remember about the key person approach and the bond of attachment is that your child needs to have as few people as possible caring for him.

Why? Well remember that the available adult must know the child well and must be able to interpret the child's needs. When a child has many carers, each responding to the child differently, the child may learn to wait passively for needs to be met such as being fed and changed.

He may allow anyone to change his nappy or put him down for a nap. However, he may also have no one who is reliably and consistently 'there' for him, and to whom he can turn for comfort. When this happens a child learns to be emotionally independent (far too early) or he learns less positive ways of gaining attention. It is worth considering, therefore, how many key people your child will have during their time in nursery. High quality nurseries work hard to implement the 'key person' approach as fully as possible and work hard to ensure that this is available to each child for the majority of the time the child attends.

Consider too that if your child moves from room to room every six or 12 months this may mean that your child could have as many as eight or ten key people and/or back-up key people.

Today, it is possible to find a few nurseries were children do not have to move from room to room; where mixed age group care is available and where children are able to make long-term attachments.

Many nurseries will assign a temporary key person when your child first starts. This is because they recognise that your child may show a preference for another person. If this is the case your child should be assigned to the new person. This is good practice. You cannot choose who the key person will be as this will depend on the above and on which member of staff has capacity to take your child. However, in the event that you don't get on with the key person you may ask for a change, but if your child is happily settled with this person I would strongly recommend that both you and the key person work hard to make the relationship work for the sake of your child.

Many parents suffer pangs of guilt when they decide to leave their child in the care of another person. This guilt is sometimes compounded by the fact that the child then takes to the new person and forms a relationship with that person, looking forward to seeing her and sometimes not wanting to go home. This may make the parent feel unwanted, under-valued and unimportant. If the child is attached to the new carer, this is great news because now he will receive the best of care and he can really begin to grow, develop and flourish. This relationship, though it is an attachment, will be different in quality to the relationship you have with your child. You are still number one; the other person is always second best. Your child will probably prove this to you by being much more difficult for you than for his key person! After all you are the only person who loves him unconditionally no matter what he does; you are always there for him. So with you he gets to be himself, warts and all.

Beware if a nursery tells you, 'We don't really use the key person role here, all our children know all the staff and are happy to be changed, fed etc. by all of us'. Or they tell you, 'Oh we use it for planning and record-keeping but that's all, we all care for the children'.

This shows the nursery does not fully understand the emotional needs of the children and have not implemented the key person approach properly.

Some nurseries refer to the role as the 'key worker' this won't matter as long as their practices are correct.

To summarise:

The key person should be someone both you and your child trust.

Your child may become very attached to his key person which is a good thing.

You and the key person must work together to meet the needs of your child; sharing important information with her about your child will help.

The fewer people caring for your child, the more likely your child is to form secure attachments.

Chapter 9

On Closer Inspection

Earlier in the book I discussed what children really need. I want to think about that now in a little more detail.

Nurseries care for children in clearly defined age ranges; moving children from room to room and from key person to key person to aid the smooth running of the nursery. It is much easier to care for a small group of babies in one room than it is to have one or two babies mixing with children of three and four years of age. Each age range has specific needs, different to the one before. The resources they each need are different and methods of communication are different too. It is widely accepted that babies learn from older children and from adults of all ages. Babies able to watch and associate with older children often develop skills in all areas faster than babies who spend time with lots of other babies. Toddlers spending time with older children may play with resources not normally offered to children of their age; they may join in with a small group to listen to a story, they may be on the receiving end of play that involves sharing and turn-taking. The pre-school child will benefit enormously from spending some time with babies and toddlers as they practice empathy, sharing and care. As the 'big' child they feel confident, skilled and knowledgeable and love to share this knowledge with younger children. Ofsted have now recognised that it is good for children to mix across the age ranges and have suggested that nurseries strive to provide care that allows children to mix for some part of every day. Seek a nursery that embraces this practice.

As we have stated, babies learn by spending time with children and people from all age ranges. They learn from being close to warm, nurturing adults and by being exposed to a wealth of stimulating, repetitive experiences. Let us begin by imaging what a Baby Room, in an average sized nursery, might look like. Perhaps there will be nine babies, usually from six to 18 months with three adult members of staff. This is quite a realistic picture as I have witnessed as many as 15 babies of this age range with five adults all in one room.

Let us think about what that might feel like for a baby, the noise, sights, smells and sounds. It will almost certainly not feel like or replicate the home life of the baby. That is the first thing to consider and, whilst it is not essential for the nursery to look like or feel like home, it is easier for the baby to adapt to conditions which are most like home. To understand this we need to consider the stage of development for children under two years of age. According to Jean Piaget, there are four stages of cognitive development. When thinking about babies we consider the 'sensory-motor stage' to be from birth to two years. During this stage of development babies are constantly learning new things through a process of assimilation. Any new experience or learning brings about disequilibrium and confusion. As the experience becomes familiar there is 'accommodation'; a sort of expansion of learning.

Babies will, over time, adapt behaviours to accommodate the new learning. There is now a state of equilibrium. You can imagine, therefore, that babies are in a constant state of assimilation, accommodation and adaptation. Ideally, experience of nursery life will be positive and as close to a warm and nurturing experience as the baby currently knows.

It is likely that the baby's current experience is that when they cry, they are the only baby that cries and their cries/needs are met by a kind, experienced care giver. What might it be like for a baby, on entering nursery, to hear lots of other babies crying? Babies are labile; that is to say that their moods are fluctuating, they copy the emotions of those around them. If one baby cries almost all the other babies will cry too. Whilst this is normal, and there may be nothing wrong with the other eight babies in the room, it is noisy and hard to listen to. More than that, of course, is how to stop them all crying? Of course, at home when the baby cries you can pick him up. In day care, with a ratio of one adult to three babies how can this be achieved? Consider, therefore, that nurseries operating on lower ratios of children to adults will be able to offer babies and older children the greatest opportunities for emotional security and learning.

As the majority of nurseries care for children in clearly identified age ranges, for ease of reading, I have divided the next chapters into rooms for specific age ranges.

The following descriptions detail what can reasonably be expected of nurseries where practice is 'outstanding'.

Parents may use these chapters to assess the level of care and learning opportunities currently being provided for their child. Day care providers may wish to use the following chapters as a self-assessment tool.

Where this is the case, I strongly suggest that the management team work together with staff to make an honest assessment under each of the headings. I have provided tables, at the end of the book which day care providers may find useful. The completed tables will then provide you with an action plan. Setting realistic target dates will make goals more achievable.

This table is similar in format to the one I currently use when carrying out a private inspection for nurseries wishing to provide or move to 'outstanding' practice.

There are three categories for each room, firstly **'Toys, Resources and Furniture', secondly 'Play and Learning Opportunities' and lastly 'Staff.'**

I will focus on three different rooms in the nursery, these are **Baby Room** covering the age range birth - 18 months. **Toddler Room** 18 months to three years and the **Pre-school Room** three - five years. Each has its' own chapter in this book.

Of course, the nursery will probably have names for these rooms such as, Bluebell, Buttercup and Daffodil, I have given general age ranges so that you can identify to which room I refer.

Chapter 10

The Baby Room

Babies need warm, caring and reliable adults on whom they can depend. They need to spend time with people who will cater for their need to explore but who understand their need for the company of the adult. They need time to discover the things of their world and to learn about people. They need to see other children and to watch them at play. Babies love songs and stories and will imitate the actions of others. They show delight in the praises of others and are upset by the tears and sounds of unhappy children. From birth the babies first play-thing is the adult; they will investigate the parent's body, putting their fingers in a parent's mouth, taking off glasses and reaching for earrings or hair as they try to discover, 'Where do you end and I begin?'. Under five months of age babies are happily engaged by the company of adults needing few play-things but happy when they have another person in view. Babies cry to have their needs met and need adults who are able to interpret their gestures and cries.

Toys, Resources and Furniture:

The baby room should be a cosy and comfortable room with priority given to creating a nurturing environment for babies. There should be an adult-sized chair in which staff can sit to nurse and feed babies. There must be clean carpets and soft furnishings such as rugs and cushions. There will be highchairs for babies to be fed in as well as a range of low reclining chairs. The floors must be clean and staff should not wear outdoor shoes in this room. Visitors and other staff should be asked to remove their shoes on entering as babies will spend much of their time on the floor.

There should be a range of small toys, some of which will be musical and of the right size for small hands to hold. There should be equipment suitable for small children to pull themselves up against and enough floor space for babies who are learning to walk and crawl. Where it is not easy to get babies out several times a day there should be opportunities for large play equipment to be brought into the room for children to practice climbing, balancing, holding and sliding.

There should be a place, this may be a peg, on which to hang a bag, or a tray, for each child's personal equipment.

There should be a number of cots, travel-cots are acceptable, for small children to sleep in. Children do not routinely sleep in reclining chairs. Pushchairs are sometimes used for children to sleep in but this should only be as a last resort for a child who will not sleep in a cot to nap.

Each cot should have clean bed linen that is changed for each child's use. The cots should be placed in a quiet area of the room where lighting can be dimmed, not dark. Staff should monitor sleeping children every ten minutes and record doing so.

The baby room should have easy access to a milk kitchen and a changing room/area.

The room should have a range of natural materials, such as *treasure basket play and large and small mirrors should be available for babies to see themselves in. Music should not be used in the background but should be used for a specific purpose, such as an accompaniment to singing, as small children need to hear other people speaking in order to learn to speak.

Play and Learning Opportunities:

Babies should be provided with opportunities to play on the floor supported by cushions and with adults available to play nearby. The baby room should have a wide range of interesting materials that will stimulate all of the senses. This cannot be done by providing only plastic toys. Babies will need to be provided with opportunities to go outside every day, even in winter. This is achieved by taking children out, well wrapped-up, in their pushchairs to watch other children at play. Babies should have facilities outside where they can watch other children playing, but are safe from the foot traffic of bigger children. Babies need to be able to dig, climb, push, pull, balance, swing and discover. They need to have shelter from the sun, wind and rain. Babies need to have opportunities to see older children playing and to mix with others sometimes.

Babies should be provided with play using a range of messy materials which will promote their sensory skills. They should have access to sand, water, paint and mark-making materials as well as opportunities to play with pasta, gloop, shredded paper and rice or lentils.

Babies need opportunities to share books with adults. They need to be provided with a cosy corner where they can play or sit undisturbed by the foot traffic of others as they investigate materials.

Television is NOT used in this room.

Treasure basket play is provided by giving a child a large natural basket filled with safe and natural objects from around the home.

Staff:

Babies need adults who understand them and their needs well. Adults who work with babies should be experienced and suitably qualified. Staff must respond to the needs of the baby kindly and gently. They must be able to move non-mobile babies from one place to another to provide them with a different view of the world. Staff should provide consistency of care and routine and should not move from one room to another to suit the running of the nursery. The attachment needs of the children are always a priority.

Staff should treat all babies fairly according to their individual needs and must not favour some children whilst leaving others out. Staff should spend time reading to and singing with babies, sharing books and toys together.

Staff must never leave babies crying or upset and must not shout at babies. Staff must understand that babies need attention and do not expect them to be content with one or two toys for long periods of time. Staff should feed babies by holding them if, bottle fed, or spoon-feed their own key children. Staff should talk to babies when feeding them and throughout their care routines. Babies must be allowed to sleep as they need and staff must not wake sleeping babies to suit the running of the nursery or routines.

Staff should change their key children's nappies whenever it is possible and should not operate a 'conveyor belt' system which is one member of staff changes all nappies.

Staff must be scrupulous in their hygiene standards when feeding and changing babies. They must wear an apron to serve meals and a different one for nappy changes, staff must always wear gloves to change nappies.

Chapter 11

The Toddler Room

The toddler room should reflect the very different needs of children of this age.

Toddlers are moving out of babyhood and are becoming intrepid explorers. They are desperate to find out about the things of their world. They want to find out, 'How does this work, what can it do?' and, 'What happens when I do this?'. They are driven physically and intellectually to discover. They are much more physically active, as they are rapidly learning new skills as well as refining existing skills. Their language is becoming more discernible but they will often be frustrated by their inability to make others understand. They are able to use more complex gestures and signs.

Toys, Resources and Furniture:

The room should be arranged with clear areas for play, sleep and quieter activities. These children need a room that continues to have a strong emphasis on nurture but now with more toys and activities for physical, creative and investigative play. This is done by creating distinct areas or zones which are generally enclosed on three sides. Using furniture such as book-cases, rugs and storage shelves, small areas for play can be created.

Toys allow an element of challenge and discovery and include natural materials and *heuristic play items. Resources and furniture should be well-maintained and robust as children of this age range are as likely to climb on a chair as a climbing frame and to throw a brick as they are to throw a ball.

*Schematic play themes are now evident and children will need materials to transport, empty, fill, shake and sort.

The walls should show displays of children's own work, not perfect displays of adult ideas. There should be photographs of children at play as well as photographs of children's families at heights children can see. Good examples of printed literacy should be evident showing correct use of lower and upper case lettering without spelling mistakes. Posters and displays should be multi-cultural reflecting the wider community and diverse needs. Television is NOT used in this room.

*Heuristic Play is play that enables a child to discover how materials/objects work or connect together.

*Schematic play themes refer to children's desire to repeat certain behaviours such as emptying and filling containers.

Play and Learning Opportunities:

A range of play materials, furniture and resources should be available every day and this is known as *continuous provision. These materials are added to, modified and changed regularly to reflect the interests of the children. Toddlers should have free access to sand, water, paint and malleable materials every day.

*Continuous provision refers to the materials, toys and activities that are always available for children.

These resources should be sited on the washable floor area and aprons for play should be available nearby. Play equipment to enhance sand, water, dough and paint should also be sited nearby. These should be in labelled boxes or on pegs so that children can help themselves.

Paint should be provided for toddlers every day and this is easily accomplished using a painting easel at the correct height. Large brushes and big sheets of paper allow toddlers to express themselves freely.

Toddlers do not need a large range of colours as they often apply paint to paper enjoying the sensory experience. More than two colours will often result in a 'brown' picture. Using one or two different colours only, which are changed every day, allows children to experience the pleasure of the colours.

Malleable materials are provided through play-dough, salt-dough, Plasticine or clay.

Quieter play activities should be sited away from messy play. A cosy book-corner, with an adult sized comfortable chair for nursing and cuddling should be available. A large range of soft furnishings such as different sized cushions for little ones to sit or rest on is ideal in the toddler room. Swathes of soft and light fabric hanging from the ceiling will help to create a cosy feel. Children should have access to a range of small and large hard-backed books which allow them to open flaps and feel textures. Books should depict other cultures and abilities as well as children and adults of different ethnicity. Books should be placed where children can self-select. Large books, for adults to read to children, may be out of reach of children but within view so that children can point to have them read. Adults should use a range of visual aids to bring stories and songs to life, such as puppets and pictures.

Children of this age have a short attention span and must not be expected to sit for circle time activities if they are unable or unwilling. Stories must not be used to 'keep children quiet' or 'out of the way' but should be valued by all staff as crucial to the language and communication development of the child.

A cosy home-corner should be arranged which allows a few small children to play at a time.

This should have a range of well-maintained wooden units comprising sink, cooker, washing machine or cupboard. There may be a selection of plastic fruit and vegetables from around the world. Pots, pans (small metal) and wooden implements should be available which can be used for imaginative play. Dolls with different skin tones and which include male and female gender should be provided. This area is well-maintained and staff should tidy the area between play sessions to encourage children to continue to use it. Recipe books, magazines, real fruit and vegetables, tea towels and wash cloths will help to make this area much more realistic.

Simple dressing-up clothes are all that are needed for this age range as they are, as yet, unable to dress themselves. Dressing-up opportunities can be provided by supplying hats, scarves, shawls and handbags for children to play with.

A large floor space is needed for construction type activities. Ideally this will be a carpeted area away from the foot traffic of others. Toddlers will play more comfortably on the floor than at the table. Materials for play should be labelled in large containers with both pictures and words which allow children to self-select. These should include materials for connecting pieces such as, Lego, Duplo, Stickle Bricks and Popoids.

Children need opportunities to play with small world materials such as train tracks, cars and garage, zoo and farm animals. Good staff recognise that small children get bored very easily with the same materials so should rotate stock whilst ensuring that there is always a choice of materials available.

Toddlers may still need to nap during the day so sleep opportunities can be provided by the use of small mats or low beds which can be put out as needed. Each child must have either, their own sheet or blanket provided from home or a clean one every day. Children must **not** be made to lie down or to sleep in large groups to suit the lunch arrangements of the nursery staff or the routines of others. Provision must be made for children to continue to play when others are sleeping without being made to 'be quiet'. Children must **not** be left to sleep on carpets or cushions that are walked upon by others, they must not be left to sleep near to the foot traffic of others or to be 'stepped over' by other people.

Toddlers need access to outdoor play for large portions of the day and should be able to go out whatever the weather. Where a door to the outside area is immediately available this should be left open for children to choose. Outdoor play supports children's learning and development across all areas of learning and development. Outdoor play should be offered in a way that is different to indoor play; it should be on a bigger scale. Children need access to materials that allow them to dig in soil, mud or compost instead of sand.

Water play may be provided, not in a tray but, by using an outdoor tap, hose or water butt. This allows children to collect and transport water. Painting activities can be provided by fixing a large sheet of Perspex to an outside wall. Near to this a blackboard and whiteboard allow for large scale mark-making. Children should also be given floor chalks to colour and draw on hard landscaping.

Toddlers should have safe places to climb, run, balance and jump as these are vital to the development of physical skills. Whilst some bumps and scrapes are a natural consequence of physical play adults must assess outdoor play spaces for acceptable risk. Physical play should be provided using slides and climbing-frames, using low logs and planks, securely fixed, can provide valuable climbing and balancing opportunities.

Trees and bushes allow toddlers to 'hide' whilst still in view of the adult, adding soft waterproof cushions under bushes or at the bottom of trees and sheets and pegs encourages den-making skills. Toddlers enjoy using tricycles and cars; these should be limited to zones to avoid other children being 'run-over'. Bikes and trikes should be part of the play offered not the only play.

Staff:

Toddlers need adults who recognise and value their drive to explore and discover.

Staff should be experienced, patient, kind and caring. They need to be willing to take time to listen as children try to make themselves understood. Staff must recognise the importance of communicating with toddlers and must be able to role-model good use of language, taking time to talk to children throughout the routines of the day. Staff must treat children kindly when they struggle and are frustrated in their quest for independence. Adults need to be energetic and enthusiastic, and able to respond quickly to the changing demands of children. Staff should observe their key children closely and often so that they can plan exciting, stimulating and challenging activities and opportunities for this group. They should understand that toddlers have days or times when they need lots of hugs and cuddles, when they need to feel special, loved and comforted. Staff should have an excellent team-working ethic as they support one another when children are demanding or difficult.

Staff should always sit at the table with their key children in small groups when they eat; helping only when needed. Staff should chat to children and may eat a small meal with the children modelling good practice and eating habits. A washable table cloth and small table decoration helps to create a more homely environment. Staff understand that children need to feed themselves and provide children with an apron to protect clothes. Staff must never ever remove children's clothes to keep them clean during meal times or for messy play (except occasionally water play) Staff should change their own key children's nappies whenever possible and work with parents to promote toilet training only when the child has shown signs of being ready (not when parents or adults decide).

Staff must be scrupulous in their hygiene practices and take care to wear aprons to serve meals and change nappies as well as washing hands after wiping noses. Staff must model and promote good hygiene practice with children encouraging them to wash their hands following nappy change, meals, snacks, messy play and brushing their teeth after meals. Staff must never wash a child's face whilst standing behind, holding their forehead or without asking a child. Warm wash cloths or wipes can be given to children so that they are allowed to practice self-help skills. Adults should gently and kindly remove excess food for children.

Staff should recognise that the routines of the day are valuable learning opportunities for toddlers.

Chapter 12

The Pre-school Room

Children at this age will be moving out of 'toddler-dom' and are becoming more independent. They need to do things for themselves as this gives them a sense of pride and achievement which is crucial to their long-term development. They need opportunities to practice new skills and to test their prepositions. Children need to be allowed to make mistakes in play and in their choices as this is how they learn. They must never be made to feel, foolish, stupid or silly in their choices or failed attempts. Kind adults provide explanations and encourage further effort. These children are curious investigators asking, why, what, when and how in their play and in their relationships with both adults and other children. They are likely to say, 'No' on occasions and may find it difficult to comply. Kind adults will give simple explanations to aid understanding, but will also apply clear boundaries and guidelines. Children will need to take responsibility for their own actions; learning to understand cause and effect.

Children of this age learn by doing rather than by being told. They need to practice, touch, see, feel, smell and hear to learn. They cannot learn only by sitting quietly listening or watching. They are active and enthusiastic; developing a sense of humour and fun. They form early friendships which are simple and uncomplicated, but important to them.

All those who work with this age range must appreciate that, though the children are coming to the end of their time in nursery, they are still very much little children with much to learn at the hands of patient and caring adults.

Toys, Resources and Furniture:

This room must be designed for play, learning and free choice. There should be a cosy book-corner where children can sit quietly or in groups to read or to be read to. There should be a mix of resources which are natural, wooden and plastic and are clean and well-maintained. Sufficient materials should be available for the number of children and to allow staff to rotate stock.

All toys and equipment should be labelled using words and pictures, and good examples of printed literacy should be evident throughout.

Wall displays should show children's own work which has been annotated to describe the learning story children made to achieve the end product. Photographs of children at work should be clearly labelled with descriptions and names. The room should be divided into distinct areas of play using floor coverings, bookcases and shelving units. Labelling and organisation of the materials and resources encourages and respects children as autonomous learners and readers. Each child needs a clearly labelled place for his or her own things. Children should be encouraged to participate in maintaining the environment through appropriate use of signage and adult involvement. The code of conduct, taken directly from the behaviour policy document and using developmentally appropriate language, should be clearly visible and children should participate in drawing this up. A planning board for use by staff should be visible showing the clear process of planning, beginning with observation and on to analysis and assessment and planning. Signs on the walls or hanging from the ceiling can be used to indicate each of the areas of continuous provision.

The toilet area should be accessible so that children do not have to ask to use the toilet with written signs to remind children of good hygiene practice.

Play and Learning Opportunities:

Pre-school children need opportunities to practice new skills and refine existing ones and a large part of this will involve making choices. When children are respected as autonomous learners and are encouraged to initiate play activities then they become skillful decision-makers, they grow in confidence and self-assurance. They learn to respect themselves and, in turn, to respect others. They also learn, bit by bit, to take responsibility for their own actions which is sometimes a painful process.

Children should have access to continuous provision which supports all areas of learning and development.

The resources to accompany each of these areas will need to promote and allow for opportunities to investigate, discover, question and analyse.

Sand and water play provide opportunities for children to problem-solve and use mathematical language. Funnels, water-wheels, cups, beakers and sieves encourage problem-solving and reasoning. Paint and use of malleable material provide children with an opportunity to make their own marks and practice emergent writing skills. Using brushes, sponges, printing equipment, stamps and cutters encourages children to work creatively and not simply to reproduce the adults' idea of art.

A workshop area can be set up to provide children with a range of more unusual materials for creating models and constructing their own ideas. These include scissors, Sellotape, nuts and bolts, small hammer and nails as well as soft wood such as Balsa or Cork. There should be a large collection of recycled materials which can be cut and used as required. Glue and glue-sticks allow for independence, but a glue-gun, which only adults can use, and which is kept out of reach, allows children to make large and complicated constructions with only a little help.

A cosy book-corner provides opportunities for children to sit and read quietly to each other or to themselves. Children should never be made to choose a book and sit quietly because adults are busy. Books and stories should be valued by all adults and used as a source of reference, interest and imagination by both adults and children and show a wide range of abilities and ethnicity. The book area may be used for circle time or small group discussions where children will have the opportunity to be listened to as well as listening to others for a short period of time. Mark-making materials placed nearby will allow children to practice writing skills or picture drawing inspired by books.

A floor space, with rug or carpet can be separated off for children to use indoor construction materials free from the foot traffic of others. Cars and car-mat, trains and track or small world materials should also be given a designated space on a carpet area. This is preferable to using tables as this confines play to a smaller area.

Table top toys and activities should be available near to tables and chairs so that children are able to understand the policy of, get, use, return, or lose resources.

Adults and children throughout the nursery should take care of all resources.

A home-corner should be set up which is very well resourced using materials from different cultural and ethnic groups. Additional materials may be added or changed daily. This area may be changed for different kinds of role-play. Staff should understand the value of this and should not try to introduce children to themes or topics for which they have no real experience; rather role-play should be used to support childrens' experiences and learning.

Meal times for this group are an opportunity for children to serve themselves, make choices about what and how much to eat. Children should be allowed to lay the table and to help to clear away. The adults should sit with children, modelling good practice and using the opportunity to chat.

Staff should understand that this is a routine which provides valuable learning opportunities so does not have to be rushed through to make way for activities.

Television is rarely/never used as it has little value in children's learning and play at this age.

Outdoor play experiences should be planned for and staff should utilise the available space well. Areas for play may be set up, but children should take the lead in how these areas are resourced and used. All areas of learning and development are supported through outdoor play. Children of this age enjoy and learn through digging, planting, watering, growing and harvesting as they are now more able and willing to defer pleasure for a little while; not always needing instant gratification. All areas of continuous provision should be met outside but this will need to be on a grander, bigger and more creative scale.

Plastic toys have little value in the outside space.

Staff:

Caring adults allow children to learn by being actively involved and allowing them to make decisions and choices. Adults must value children's opinions and choices, never making them feel humiliated or ashamed of their choices or 'rubbing it better' by fixing the problem. The knowledgeable adult provides the child with an opportunity to think through the problem, to come up with their own solutions or aids decision making by providing a range of scenarios for discussion or choice.

Staff working with this age range should encourage and value children as participators rather than spectators on nursery life. They understand that every child is a person in their own right and, as such, is a citizen with entitlements. Adults must not judge, criticize or mock children's use of language or behaviours, but kindly help children to reach decisions and judgements of their own. Children should be helped by the adults to manage their own behaviour, learning self-control because they have the freedom to express their feelings. Adults must work together to lay down moral codes and boundaries that show respect for all faiths, religions and practices. Adults should be well informed about other ethnic, cultural and religious practices and share this equally with children.

The key person approach must be used but this role is much more about supporting children to do things for themselves and providing a willing ear and ready hug, when needed, for this age range.

The adults should work together to plan exciting and stimulating activities for children, but the starting point for this is key people knowing their children well. Staff must observe their key children, and others, across different contexts. Analysis should be based on observations carried out over a period of time. Staff need to use this information to make an assessment of the child's learning and in planning future learning opportunities.

Staff should be flexible and respond to spontaneously occurring events as well as valuing and using the experiences the children and families bring to the nursery.

Staff should chart children's learning through the use of learning stories and in the learning journey. Staff should support one another in continued professional development.

Chapter 13

Self-Assessment Resources for Settings

The following self-assessment tables have been designed by me for the use of experienced child care practitioners or managers. They will help you to see your setting from the parents' or outsiders' view and should be used as a diagnostic tool to assess the current situation.

Tables for Self-Assessment for Day Care Providers

………………………Room   Date………………..............

The statements identify best practice as identified by the Early Years Foundation Stage (EYFS) Principles and Safeguarding Children procedures. I have also included statements which I believe are key elements of effective practice which contribute to an outstanding experience of nursery life for all children.

The rating value is used merely as a guideline to help you to identify, firstly, the changes you may wish to make to improve the experience of children and, secondly, any good practice you currently have and on which you can build.

1: Outstanding, 2: Good, 3: Requires Improvement.

Enabling Environments	Rate
The walls are clean and well-painted.	
The floors have washable areas and some carpets and cushions for children to sit on.	
The lighting and ventilation of the room is good and staff can easily adjust the temperature.	
The walls show displays of children's work which is well-labelled and tells adults and children about the display.	
There are good examples of printed literacy for children to see.	
Words and labelling is shown in more than one language. Pictorial timetable is used.	
Words and signs are spelt correctly with proper use of upper case and lower case letters.	

Furniture is clean and well-maintained.	
Areas of the room are separated for play using carpets, flooring or furniture.	
Auditory stimulation is provided for children to listen and or respond to and not for background use.	
Resources and furniture is labelled clearly for children. Pictures are used, as well as words, in the Baby and Toddler Rooms.	
Photographs of children and their families are clearly displayed at heights that can be enjoyed by children.	
Practitioners do not wear outdoor shoes in the Baby Room and all visitors are asked to remove theirs.	

Planning, fire evacuation procedures, notices and toy cleaning rota are displayed.	
The physical indoor environment offers the right balance of challenge and success to children, through the materials available and opportunities to choose.	
The physical environment allows children to 'get, use, return or lose' equipment or resources.	
Children are able to access toilet and hand-washing facilities when needed.	
Each child is provided with a space for personal belongings.	
Walls, equipment and resources stimulate children's curiosity about the world.	

Positive Relationships	Rate
The key person system is used to provide the continuity of care for children.	
Practitioners understand the key person approach and use this when carrying out all intimate care routines for children.	
A back-up key person system is used to provide emotional security for children.	
Practitioners spend time with their key children, talking and listening to them.	
Practitioners take the time to tell babies and small children what is happening to them during intimate care routines.	
Children are free to express their emotions and are provided with opportunities to do so.	
Practitioners spend time reading and singing to children.	

Practitioners take account of the needs of children by changing the routines to meet their needs.	
Practitioners respond to unwanted behaviour in gentle and supportive ways.	
Practitioners have a range of ways to deal with unwanted behaviour.	
Children are praised and rewarded by adults.	
Adults are good role models.	
Practitioners value and recognize the faith, ethnicity and religious beliefs of the child and family.	
Adults show appropriate affection for children.	
Touches and cuddles are appropriate and instigated by children.	

Practitioners spend time observing children.	
Observations are used and analysed to assess the development of children.	
Observations are used to plan activities for children and to meet the individual needs of the child.	
Children know and are reminded of appropriate ways to behave.	
Practitioners welcome all parents.	
Practitioners value the role of parents and share information daily.	
Information-sharing is valued as a two-way system, for which there is a procedure.	
Practitioners provide opportunities for parents to discuss the needs of their child in private.	

| Practitioners use appropriate methods of communicating with parents according to their language, ethnic or religious needs. | |

Learning and Development	Rate
A place to lie, rest or sit is provided for babies and or small children.	
Adequate space is provided for children who are learning to crawl or walk.	
Mobiles are used to engage babies.	
Treasure baskets and heuristic play is available.	
Large toys are available for children to practice gross motor skills.	
Practitioners move babies and toddlers to provide them with a new or different view of the world.	
Babies and toddlers are responded to quickly.	

Outdoor play is used for all children.	
Children access outdoor play more than once each day.	
Toddlers and other children are offered continuous provision in respect of: • Dough • Painting • Sand • Water • Books • Imaginative play • Role-play/home corner • Construction and small world • Mark-making Adults regularly enhance the continuous provision.	

Babies have opportunities to play with the above materials as part of daily, adult-led activities or continuous provision where possible.	
The room layout allows for children to become engrossed in individual or small group activities free from distraction.	
Children have time to become engaged in free flow play.	
Children have opportunities to become engrossed in play in a place that is free from foot traffic.	
Practitioners plan activities that help children to develop autonomy and resilience.	
Practitioners give support that is structured and appropriate for vulnerable children or those with special educational needs.	
Activities are planned that promote emotional, spiritual and social needs of the children.	

Practitioners are sensitive to the needs of the child and know when to intervene and when to observe.	
Practitioners understand the need to assess children through activities which are chosen by the child and when the child is actively engaged.	

The Unique Child	Rate
Children's own language is valued and respected.	
Practitioners take the time to find out about each child's language needs.	
Where necessary, practitioners learn new words, of a language different to their own, to communicate with the child/family.	
Practitioners use a variety of ways, including pictures or signs to communicate with children or families who do not have English as their first language.	
Practitioners understand that each child develops at a different pace and are able to offer play and learning to meet the individual needs of the child.	
Practitioners take an interest in how children think and feel which is demonstrated in their attitudes and planning.	

Practitioners encourage children and parents to bring materials and artefacts from their home to show to other children.	
Materials, books, posters and toys all show a range of abilities, ethnic origins and faiths.	
Practitioners take time to find out about the important events in children's life, including cultural celebrations.	
The environment allows children with special educational needs to participate.	
Children are not excluded, unnecessarily, from spending time one-to-one for additional support.	
Practitioners challenge discrimination in a sensitive way.	
Babies and toddlers are provided with opportunities to see and play with or be near older children.	

Children who have siblings in the setting are allowed to spend time together and to offer comfort and support to one another when needed.	
Children whose behaviour is challenging are not labelled.	
A settling-in routine is described in detail to the parents and its' importance is understood and valued by all.	
Children are not left by parents in a stressful condition.	
Practitioners encourage parents to say goodbye to children and not to 'sneak off'.	
Children are allowed to use comfort objects whilst they are settling-in.	

Additional Statements of Good Practice

Good Practice for Sleeping Children	Rate
Babies' cots are spaced three feet apart so that sleeping infants do not breathe on one another.	
Bedding is changed between each baby (this should be standard, rather than best practice).	
A ten or 15 minute checking system is in place for sleeping children and is clearly displayed and marked.	
Children are not expected to lie down or sleep when they are not tired or do not want to.	
Lighting is dim, but not dark, for sleeping children.	
Ratios till apply when children are sleeping.	
Children who do not want to sleep are offered play opportunities and not expected to be silent.	

Good Practice at Meal Times	Rate
Babies are fed whilst being held by the key person whenever possible.	
Babies who are spoon-fed are fed by their key person.	
Practitioners sit at the table with their key children.	
Older children may choose to sit with their friends for meals.	
Children are able to feed themselves whenever possible.	
Children are praised for feeding themselves, even when this is messy.	
Tables are attractively laid at meal times.	
Children are allowed to choose portion size and food preferences are respected.	

Children are given sufficient time to finish their meals.	
Practitioners do not touch or handle children's food inappropriately.	
Practitioners ask before cutting or serving food.	
Practitioners serve food at the table to children whilst discussing the content. Pre-school children serve themselves and are helped if needed.	
Practitioners encourage conversation and demonstrate good manners.	
Meal times are sociable occasions.	

Health, Hygiene and Safety	Rate
Practitioners wash their hands after wiping children's noses.	
Practitioners wash their hands after wiping their own nose.	
Practitioners dispose of all tissues immediately.	
Practitioners always wear apron and gloves when changing nappies.	
A nappy change procedure is in place and is displayed clearly on the wall.	
Cleaning materials are provided for the nappy change area. These are kept out of reach of children.	
Practitioners demonstrate a healthy attitude to the bodily functions of the child.	

Practitioners wash tables and chairs after use.	
Practitioners wear aprons to serve meals.	
Records of child's meals and hygiene needs are kept and shared with parents.	
Small children are given a clean bib for each meal.	
Older children are given a napkin and know how to use it.	
Children are given utensils to eat with which are appropriate to their age and stage of development.	
Additional or other staff provide cover for meal times and breaks in line with ratios.	
Children have a clean face cloth or individual wipe, after each meal or snack. These are washed before re-use.	

Hygiene requirements are discussed with children.	
Children know why they wash their hands.	
Children are allowed and encouraged to wash their own hands and face.	
Children are encouraged to wash their hands after messy play, outdoor play and sand play.	
Children who are ill are kept separate from other children whilst waiting to be collected by parents/carers.	
Practitioners demonstrate a good understanding of infection control measures.	
Ratios conform to Ofsted requirements at all times.	

All doors to the outside area are child-proof.	
Practitioners carry out checks on the outdoor play area before children go out. Doors to the play area are kept open and children can choose to play outside or in.	
Fences and gates are locked and maintained.	
Practitioners know the identity of adults collecting children.	

Chapter 14

Additional Information

Welfare Standards:

There are welfare standards which nurseries, playgroups, pre-schools and childminders must take account of when providing care/education for children from birth to five years.

Early Years Foundation Stage (EYFS):

This is a new framework which came into effect from September 2008 and was subsequently updated in 2014.

All private, voluntary and school establishments must take account of the framework when providing care for children birth - five years of age. They will need to demonstrate to Ofsted that children are being cared for and supported within the guidelines of the framework. In Wales the framework is called Early Years Foundation Phase (EYFP) and includes the need to promote bilingualism for all children.

Early Years Foundation Stage (EYFS), revised September 2014, is divided into two distinct parts. The first, the statutory guidance lays down the legal requirements which providers must put in place when providing either a childminding service or nursery education for children from birth to five years.

The second part of the EYFS is non-statutory, but is considered best practice to use it. This section is called the early years outcomes and details the different stages of development and learning that may typically be observed when caring for children.

The areas of learning and development are divided into the three prime areas:

- Personal, social and emotional development,
- Communication and language,
- Physical development.

There are a further four specific areas:

- Literacy,
- Mathematics,
- Understanding the world,
- Expressive art and design.

All children must make progress in the prime areas and practitioners working with babies and very young children will support the prime areas as a priority. As a child settles into nursery life, grows and develops then practitioners will take account of the four specific areas when planning activities, making observations and when carrying out assessments of learning.

Different settings will observe, plan and assess children in a variety of ways; there is no one set way in which this must be done. The documentation used to plan, observe and assess children should be shared with parents on a regular basis and, of course, you may ask to see this at any time.

Treasure Basket Play:

Elinor Goldschmied is the proponent of treasure baskets. In her work with children in day care she noted children were less interested in plastic toys and manufactured objects for children. She noted how they would happily play for much longer periods with ordinary household objects which appealed to children's senses. They were stimulating to touch, to feel with the tongue, the sound was interesting when they were clanged and hit together, they did not smell like plastic toys and they were more visually interesting.

A treasure basket should be a wide-based natural wicker-type basket which contains a wide range of sensory materials normally found around the home. These objects, not normally given to babies and small children, are safe because the adult stays near to the baby whilst they play. All the objects should be things which a baby can safely 'mouth', but cannot swallow. The basket is given to non-mobile babies only. Once a baby can walk the materials may be of less interest as the child is now interested in his environment. Also some of the materials would be less safe to a baby who is walking and, therefore, may fall whilst 'mouthing' an object. Here are some objects you may include in a basket;

- Wooden spoons
- Wooden lemon squeezer
- Wooden honey-spoon
- Metal pan
- Metal spoons

- Bunch of keys
- Chamois leather
- Dish cloth and sponge
- A lemon
- Small sieve
- C.D.
- A short length of heavy chain

It is important to remember that all of these items may represent a hazard to small children if they are left alone with them. The role of the adult is to provide the basket with interesting objects in and to stay close as the child investigates the materials for themselves. Never leave a baby with a treasure basket and never include anything that you feel is unsafe.

Heuristic Play:

This type of play is about 'discovery'. The word comes from the Greek word 'Eurisko' meaning 'Eureka!' - 'I have discovered something.' This type of play is a direct follow-on from treasure basket play. The emphasis though is different; previously materials were sought which allowed a baby to learn through their senses, now the adult provides materials which fit together or which can connect.

These materials are normally recycled objects from around the home. Toddlers from 18 months to three years enjoy this type of play most, but I have seen children as old as six and eight years of age using heuristic materials in imaginative ways.

Small children may spend long periods of time engaged in emptying and filling containers, moving items from one place to another, stirring, pushing, wrapping or sorting materials. This play is known as 'schematic' play meaning repeatable patterns of behaviour. Heuristic play materials allow children to repeat actions in their play.

Here is a list of the materials you may wish to include, but note that now there may be small pieces. These should only be included once children have ceased 'mouthing':

- A range of large and small plastic bottles with lids
- Yoghurt pots
- Cream pots or tubs with lids
- Unused corks
- Large buttons
- Large polished pebbles or stones
- Wooden pegs both the spring and the dolly type
- Large tins (such as for biscuits or chocolates) with lids
- Small tins with lids such as for baby milk or custard powder
- Small buckets or metal plant pots
- Sieves and funnels
- Long pieces of chain (half metre)
- Long pieces of tubing, such as hose pipe or clear tube

You can include baked bean or tuna tins but these must be washed, labels removed and the sharp edges double wrapped with parcel tape or sticking plaster tape

Please remember that with all of these materials it is the job of the adult to manage health and safety. Do not leave children alone with heuristic play materials.

If in doubt leave it out!

Mouthing:

This is a natural and essential stage of development. All children from a few months of age will put, first, their fingers and, then, any object they can get hold of into their mouth. Adults caring for children need to make sure that babies have the opportunity to 'mouth' objects, making sure that materials within the baby's grasp are not too small to present a choking hazard. Mouthing allows children to feel and to taste objects and to discover more about them as the tongue is one of the most sensitive organs we have. Babies who are not allowed to put things into their mouth may feel confused and frustrated. 'Mouthing' will help babies who are teething to 'cut' their teeth and they can be offered welcome relief by being given a cold object, which has been kept in the refrigerator, to 'mouth'. Babies will stop 'mouthing' anywhere between the age of 12 and 24 months. Children who were not allowed to 'mouth' objects as a baby may continue to put things in their mouth long after this time.

Pictorial Timetable

This is a timetable in pictures that is clearly visible on the walls in each nursery room. It will show the key routines of the day in photographic form. Pictures of children arriving, playing, eating snacks or meals, napping, playing and then parents arriving to collect children can all be included. This is a useful tool in helping children who are unhappy, do not have English as a first language or are too young to understand the passage of time.

Schematic Play:

This is a fascinating topic, though rather long to discuss in detail here. I cover this in more depth in my next book, 'The Language of the Baby'.

Schemas are 'repeatable patterns of behaviour' they are most often seen in the play of small children from six months to five years of age. Put simply schemas are demonstrated in the types of play children prefer most; they are seen in the tools they use and the methods they employ to carry out their play. Schemas are trans-global, meaning that children all across the world will demonstrate the same particular types of play. Schemas are natural and children should be supported in their schematic play, this means that the adult's role is to ensure that the desire/need for schematic play can be fulfilled. When children are thwarted in developing or completing schematic play this can lead to what might be seen as bad behaviour. A child's interest in a specific schema may last for a very long time or be fulfilled through a relatively short play experience of just a few hours or days. Whilst it is not necessary to identify the type of schema, knowledgeable practitioners should look for examples of schematic play and support children's interest by providing resources and time for the schema to be fulfilled.

Here are a few examples of schematic play, the list is not exhaustive:

- Posting - a desire to post objects into and through other things.
- Envelopment - completely covering an item, this is usually observed in children's drawings and paintings. They will paint a lovely picture and then completely cover it over with paint. The original painting cannot be seen.
- Containment -putting things into boxes, bags and other containers.
- Compartmentalising - order, pattern, separating and organising by group, colour or size.
- Core and radial schema - stirring, watching the water go around and down the toilet or sink.
- Horizontal - making long lines of things.
- Vertical - making towers.

Chapter 15

Childminders

To register with the LA the childminder will have to state how he/she will provide care and learning for all children in their care. Childminders are subject to the EYFS and will need to demonstrate to Ofsted how they support children's development and learning in each of the areas. They are subject to regular inspections from Ofsted. Some childminders may work in partnership with another registered minder in their own home whilst others may employ another person to assist them. Although most minders work alone, good minders will belong to a local childminding network group and many will be members of The National Childminding Association (NCMA). All minders must have insurance to care and work in their own home and they must have specific cover to carry children in their car. Childminders do not have to have a childcare qualification, but must have attended a local authority run training course. Many good minders study and take a nationally recognised qualification in home-based care.

As part of my research for this book I have been very fortunate in being invited into the homes of childminders. Many years ago, when my own children were small I was a registered childminder and was lucky to work with some lovely parents and children. I did this at a time when I wanted to remain at home with my own children and was very much in need of some extra income. However, I felt that if I wrote the book purely from my own experience of minding then it would not be balanced or current. Childminding today is very different to the role I had more than twenty years ago. Childminding is a business; childminders are subject to Ofsted inspection and must apply the Early Years Foundation Stage (EYFS) to their practice. Like nurseries, the childminding setting and the childminder will vary enormously. I have tried to give the reader a detailed description of what you should see in the very best of childminding homes; what is considered good practice and what is not. What appears to be most common is that many people, mainly women, start childminding because they have a child of their own and do not want to return to work, but may need to contribute to the family income. Many of the minders I met had continued to mind long after their own child had started school or even grown-up and moved out. Many of the men I have met, either whilst training childminders or on visits to their homes, were minding as part of a partnership with their wives. Some men are minders in their own right having chosen to make a career change.

When embarking on the choice of day care it is very worthwhile visiting a number of nurseries and childminders.

What can you expect when you visit a childminder?

It is likely that just one person will care for your child every day. You will need to feel that you trust this person, that they are kind, organised, well-ordered and that they are professional in their business dealings with you. The minder is subject to strict regulations and will be able to prove that they are registered to care for children in their own home. It is not possible for me to say what the environment should look like as there are as many different homes as there are people living in them, and this book is about choosing nursery care, but the following bullet points may help you. When visiting the childminder look for:

- A wide range of good quality toys and equipment for children of all ages.
- A clean, hygienic, organised home.
- Plenty of space for children to play both indoors and out.
- A clean, organised, safe outdoor space that is easily accessed by children.
- Any pets are kept clean, healthy and are friendly to visitors.

Ask to see the following:

- Ofsted registration documents
- Insurance documents
- Planning and assessment documents for all children
- A learning journey
- A copy of the Data Barring Service (DBS) certificate for every person resident in the home over sixteen years of age.

What is most important is that you feel that the person you meet is kind and loving and that you feel able to have a warm relationship with that person yourself.

Chapter 16

Messy Play at Home

Offering children the opportunity to play with a range of creative materials such as paint, sand, water and dough in your own home may at first seem 'a step too far' for some parents/carers, but let us examine how these materials can be provided to support your child's learning and development at home without too much mess.

If you are at home you can offer your child stimulating play materials that are different to the ones that a nursery will offer but which will be just as valuable.

You can show your child how to use the materials and resources from around his own home and he will learn new skills at your side.

A word of advice, whatever your child is playing with will only be interesting to him if he has an adult nearby to chat to and to help with good ideas, if he has run out of new ways to play. If you leave him alone in a room with the materials, his play will not last or he may decide to use the materials in a way they weren't designed for, i.e drawing on the walls, cutting his own hair or sticking the paper pieces to the dog's tail.

Whilst your child is playing you don't need to do anything other than comment on what he has done, 'Wow that looks great, I love the colour'. You don't need to ask, 'What is it?' as small children often paint and create just for the sensory pleasure and not with a specific purpose in mind.

Do not be tempted to do it for him, 'Here let me show you'. So very often adults take over showing children how to, 'cut out neatly', stick bits on, 'in the right place' or making it look 'better'. This will make the child feel as though his work is not good enough. Be available to help only if you are asked, sit on your hands and let him do it his way. Remember children learn by 'doing' not by watching others do.

Sand/Digging:

Sand is provided in nursery for children to play with as it is a clean material for digging in. Twenty or 30 years ago most of us would have grown up playing in the street, back-yard or garden where we would have had ample opportunity to dig in the soil to make mud pies. But many children do not play in the garden, street or back-yard as they spend many of their waking hours away from home and in nursery care. If you are caring for your child at home you do not have to provide sand for your child to dig in if you are able to offer any type of outside play space.

Providing opportunities for digging can be achieved in the following ways:

Garden:

If you have a garden leave a small patch of soil where your child can dig. Always check the area before your child plays for animal faeces.

Garden forks and trowels are too large for children to hold and the child sized ones can be expensive so provide large and small spoons and forks and small plastic plant pots or yoghurt pots for emptying and filling.

Yard Area:

Buy a grow-bag and a large sheet of heavy-duty plastic. Lay the plastic under the grow-bag and make a small circular hole in the top. Provide materials as above.

When your child has finished playing scoop the soil back into the grow bag and cover with the plastic sheeting to stop animals using the area as a toilet.

Small Patio or Balcony:

As above.

Varying the Play:

You may vary play opportunities by using small buckets and tubs so that the child can empty and fill from the grow-bag or ground into a range of vessels.

Keep a small set of toys which are just used for outdoor play such as:

- Plastic animals
- Cars and trucks
- Building blocks.

No Outside Space:

If you have no space out-of-doors for your child to play, but would still like to provide digging opportunities, you can either provide a sand pit filled with sand and used in the kitchen or a room with a washable floor surface. You may provide small buckets and tubs filled with either sand or soil and spoons or forks for digging and placed on a large sheet of heavy duty plastic. This makes scooping the contents back up much easier. Other materials for indoor digging and scooping include: rice, lentils, split peas and dried pasta. These can all be provided with spoons and sieves and a large washing up bowl and smaller tubs and bowls.

Painting:

Painting is offered to children in nursery so that they may have an opportunity to 'mark-make' this literally means 'make their mark'. It is also a sensory activity which allows children to enjoy the feel of the paint on the paper and on their hands. Children can be seen making marks without the aid of pens, paper and paint. The baby in the highchair can be seen rubbing their hands around and around in the spilt milk on his tray. He is already enjoying the feel and sight of his marks.

The older child may use the spoon or fork to make whirls in his custard, gravy or the soil you provided.

You may feel that you do not want to have paint in the house in which case you can offer mark-making opportunities using crayons, chalk, pencils and paper. As a general rule the smaller the child the larger the materials will need to be. A baby of about 12 months of age will not have enough control to make marks on a piece of A5 paper with a pencil. But they will enjoy watching lines appear as they move a stubby piece of chalk across a large piece of paper. Here are some more ideas for good clean fun:

Painting in the bath; provide large cheap paint brushes for children to 'paint' the bathroom tiles whilst in the bath. Squeeze some bubble bath onto the brushes for them to 'paint' themselves.

Provide large paint brushes and tubs of water for children to 'paint' the paved areas outside.

Mix a tiny drop of food colouring into a large pot of water and provide a large paint brush and paper for baby to paint with whilst in his highchair. It won't matter if he sucks the brush.

Painting for older children. Buy powder paint as opposed to ready mixed as it is cheaper. Mix this in yoghurt pots with washing-up liquid and a small amount of water as it makes it easier to get it out of clothes and furnishings. Cover the table with a really cheap plastic cloth. I find that a used/old shower curtain is excellent for messy play. Provide large brushes and card (save cereal boxes for drawing on).

Water:

The water tray is provided in nursery because those children who spend much of their time in nursery do not have an opportunity to help with the washing-up. Small children will spend hours playing in the sink. You can often get a whole meal prepared whilst a child is happily helping with the dishes.

If your child is old enough to stand on a chair by the sink then simply ensure that the water in the bowl is just warm, add a cloth, some safe household items that won't break if dropped and are not sharp and stay close by. This is a wonderful opportunity for you and your child to 'work' together in the kitchen. Putting a large bath towel under the chair works better than a plastic sheet as it will absorb the spills better and can be popped in to the washing machine. Babies can be provided with water play just by bathing them nightly.

Gluing and Sticking:

With the wonderful invention of glue-sticks this once messy activity is now so much easier to provide at home. Children of about three years of age will really love sticking bits of recycled materials together to make a model or putting pieces onto paper. I like to have a 'rainy-day box' for when you have run out of ideas or the weather is terrible and you need to entertain a small child; this box will give them lots of fun.

Simply collect together a large shoe box and pop into it old packages, greetings cards, magazines, scissors, ribbon, gift wrap, foil, beads and buttons together with Sellotape and card or paper. Produce the box only when needed so that it doesn't lose its appeal. Now stand back and let your child do the rest. You may need to be available for help with sticky tape if your child is making a model as glue sticks aren't really designed for model making. Children of three years of age can be taught, with a little patience, to use scissors. Small scissors can be bought quite cheaply.

Dough:

Children are offered dough to play with in nursery because when most of us spent our time at home with our parents (normally mother) we would have been taught bit by bit to cook and to bake. Dough allows children to practice some of these skills. You do not need to provide dough for your child; you can simply allow him to watch and to play with the materials as you cook.

The baby in the highchair will play, very happily, with a spoon and a potato or a few pieces of pasta and a small pan whilst watching you.

Toddlers and older children can be given similar items but you may provide opportunities for him to make simple sandwiches by giving him bread and cheese or a little dish of butter and a plastic knife to spread his own. He will enjoy baking activities and you don't need to be a cook, as your child will be happy to spread a little jam or icing onto ready-made biscuits, crackers or bread rolls.

Children will love to make very simple biscuits, which they will happily eat, just provide three tablespoons of flour and a tablespoon of butter which they can mix with their fingers until it is well mixed then add a little milk to stick it together and let them roll this into little balls which they then flatten with their hands.

Pop them onto a baking sheet or foil and bake in a moderate oven until brown.

Final Words

During the time I have worked in or visited nurseries I have witnessed adults taking care of children in ways that are acceptable and, sometimes, in ways that have made me weep. I sometimes shake my head in utter disbelief at the things I have seen or heard. Many of these incidences may well have simply been absorbed by children in their general overall experience of nursery life, leaving them little-harmed by the experience.

I have not learned to live with these 'incidences' and the images do not fade with time but rather they gain clarity. Now I begin to see and understand what the problem is and to gauge the depth of it.

There is, in some parts of society, a deep disrespect for children. It resides in the homes of some families tainting the language of parents. It can be witnessed too in the behaviour and attitude of some school teachers.

It quietly and insidiously worms its way into our care of the child, it affects our behaviours and our judgements. Over time, disrespect begins to erode the spirit of the child so that eventually the child becomes like the adult, learning to disrespect the purity and golden glow of childhood.

But there is hope; through my work I have seen, met and read about people who love children, who respect them and delight in their unique, incredible, untainted vision of the world. Perhaps some of these adults exist because they too were respected as a child.

I believe that society must continue to change its' attitude to childhood; in a desire to measure, assess, manage and educate children we are in danger of reducing childhood to the smallest portion of our lives. Childhood is not preparation for life, it is life. Life in all its wonder, awe, glory and pain. Children need the adults who work with them and care for them to acknowledge the enormous privilege it is to spend time with them. I, for one, count myself blessed every day in my work with children.

Recently one of my charges told me, 'I love you more than chocolate cake with sprinkles'.

Bibliography:

Every Child Matters constituted the Government's policy response to the findings and recommendations of Lord Laming's Inquiry. It was published as a Green Paper for consultation on 8th September, 2003 concurrently with the Government's recommendation-by-recommendation response to Lord Laming's report which was published in January, 2003.

Further Information:

Learning through Landscapes website is:
www.ltl.org.uk

Forest Schools website is: **www.forestschools.com**

About the Author

Jane Smalley lectured in Childhood studies from 2000-2005 before launching NURSERYWISE, her training and consultancy service. Jane provided advice and guidance for local authorities across the north of England, supporting settings to raise the quality of education and care provided to children. Delivering training for early years teachers and practitioners and writing bespoke training packages, Jane was able to support settings to make considerable improvement.

In 2010 Jane joined a prestigious independent school where she led the nursery through a period of growth and change.

In 2013 Jane opened Shrewsbury Prepatoria, a unique preparatory school delivering the most comprehensive approach to Reggio Emilia education in the UK. Their website can be found at:

www.shrewsburyprepatoria.co.uk

Acknowledgements

Elaine Baines for the editing, proof reading, research and study you did just to get this to print, thank you.

To the many owners, managers and practitioners who allowed me access to their settings, thank you.

To my wonderful team at Shrewsbury Prepatoria for never groaning (out loud) when I say, 'I've had another great idea'!

My Next Book

If you enjoyed this book perhaps you will enjoy my next book, 'The Language of the Baby'. Here's a short extract:

So you've been pacing the floor for an hour, it's dark, it's raining outside and the house is quiet. The only sound is from the child balanced on your arm, resting against your shoulder and screaming. The tears run silently down your face and you feel as if the whole world is asleep except you. You remember the words of the midwife as you left the hospital, 'Don't worry you'll soon get to know what he wants', but you feel as if this is never going to happen. So, go back through the list you tell yourself; tick the boxes. Is he clean? Tick. Fed? Tick. Teething? Too young, tick. Tired? Yes, definitely, but will he sleep? Now you resort to singing, bouncing and pleading, 'oh please just go to sleep'!

Let's take some time now to consider just what may happening here. Crying and screaming are the language of the baby. This is the only way they can communicate their needs to the available adult; without this babies would not survive. And guess what, your job is not to stop them crying, that's right, your job is not to stop them crying, but rather to interpret the cries and to meet the need. 'OK', I hear you saying, 'That's what I'm trying do right now, I'd love to know what he wants'. But let's back the truck up a little. Don't you feel less stressed by learning that you don't have to stop your baby crying? He's communicating his needs in the only way possible so instead of stopping the crying, why don't we think about the different ways in which we can respond to his cries.

In the first weeks of life babies have just one type of cry and this is used in response to any physiological need..............................